The Techniques of
Wood Sculpture

The Techniques of
Wood Sculpture

David Orchard

North Light   Cincinnati Ohio

© David Orchard 1984
First published 1984
Reprinted 1985

Published in North America 1985 by
North Light
9933 Alliance Road
Cincinnati Ohio 45242

Library of Congress Cataloging in Publication Data

Orchard, David.
    The techniques of wood sculpture.

    Bibliography: p.
    Includes index.
    1. Sculpture—Technique.   2. Wood-carving—
Technique.   I. Title.
NB1250.073   1984   731.4'62   84–27327
ISBN 0–89134–121–8

Printed in Great Britain

Contents

Acknowledgements

The author wishes to offer his special thanks to Mrs Eleanor Clarke (widow of the late Ron Lane) for the loan of her collection. The author also wishes to thank the following: Steve Shrimpton, whose technical excellence may be seen in the colour plates; Len Hart, for other photographs and his interest and help in compiling and photographing the constructional sequences for the practical examples; Walter Mansbridge, for the loan of his bowl; John Sweetman and Tom Ruse for checking the manuscript, and Alison Bellhouse for editing it; Brian Williams, for his contribution on relief carvings; the many friends and colleagues (too numerous to mention individually) who have given their time and advice; the staff of the galleries and museums, for their courtesy and assistance; my son and daughters, for their assistance with the background research; and last but not least, my dear wife, without whose constant help and encouragement this book would not have been written.

My thanks go to the following for the use of photographs: The Tate Gallery, London (pp. 73, 80, 85 and 87); Steve Shrimpton (pp. 74 and 90); the University of Southampton and Justin Knowles (p. 91 [right]); the Dean and Chapter of Winchester Cathedral (pp. 88 and 130); The Victoria and Albert Museum, Crown Copyright (pp. 93, 115 [top] and 118); Len Hart (pp. 107, 119 and 123) and Jack Whitemore (pp. 116 and 117). The photograph on p. 81 appears by courtesy of The News Portsmouth.

There are a number of references in this book to the influence that an artist may receive from the work of another artist or a particular subject matter.

One such modern example is the work of Ron Lane who gave almost as much importance to his medium as he did to the form. He used the subtleties of the grain pattern of the timber as a source of inspiration and any peculiarity in this distinctive formation influenced his train of thought. A swirl in the grain may suggest the eye of an otter, or the figure (grain pattern) of quarter sawn timber may represent the feathers of a pheasant.

Ron was a gifted sculptor, artist and lecturer who became an influence on many people especially in the south of England. His name is a byword for excellence and lives on in the form of a memorial trust, set up in his name to encourage wood sculpture in schools. His life was full, rewarding and endowed with an appreciation of nature. He had the gift of being able to convey this in his sculpture, lectures and way of life. Ron was a man much loved for his work and willingness to give advice, whose name can only become more well known than it is at present.

The four part title photographs show works by Ron Lane.

Introduction

What is sculpture?
Sculpture is the human skill of forming representations of objects.

What is a sculptor?
A sculptor can be almost anyone with a desire to create something. Potential sculptors are often discouraged by the apparent complication of shapes and knowledge of tools and materials. In other words, they do not know how or where to start. This book is designed to aid such people, to encourage them to create in their own way whatever appeals to them.

Perhaps expense is an initial deterrent. This book points out that in fact very few tools are required to start with and it emphasises that tools should be purchased as required to cope with the work engaged in at the time. Obtaining the materials needed also requires very little or no financial outlay.

Where does one start?
Some sculptors are attracted to a particular style of work. This attraction may be due to the influence of their skills which follow a certain direction, or perhaps they have progressed through the traditional styles to the more contemporary or abstract. Whatever the reason, they all had to learn basic techniques and it is these techniques which form the foundations of this book.

Attitudes to art

It is important that one sculptor should not dismiss another's art simply because he does not understand the particular motive or method of execution applied to his works. The author shows examples of works by famous sculptors, and explains some of the possible reasons for a particular technique or material being employed. This will help to broaden the reader's understanding and appreciation of the different attitudes others might have to their art.

Choice of Material

Why do we want to carve wood when it seems so much easier to model in clay? In fact, a wood carver will use clay for his *maquettes* or rough models. He will introduce very little detail but will keep to a shape which will guide him in producing his finished work. Probably the greatest influence on the sculptor is the desire to work in a certain medium, although the strength of the material also has a bearing on the finished product. For instance, slender works will benefit from the strength of timber with the grain running in the correct direction, whilst a similar piece in clay would either have to be reinforced with wire or a supporting piece disguised into its surroundings.

The desire to work in timber is inherent in the sculptor who has an affinity with this material, in the same way that his desire prompts him to carve or construct certain types of work. He will prefer to work with a material which he finds satisfying and attractive; from the fine detail in traditional one-piece carvings, for example, to the smooth contours and simplicity of abstract works. In some cases, the sculptor might have recourse to several different materials in order to convey his artistic message.

One thing we must all realise is that Nature is the supreme sculptor and there is no way in which the human can approach such perfection, so, when working, this fact should be borne in mind. It will tell us when to stop working on the model and when enough form has been developed.

I History of Wood Sculpture

1 Origins

To research the origins of wood sculpture, it is necessary to look into the subject of sculpture in a more general sense. Timber, being an organic material, has left us with few examples and, because of this, it has to be assumed that the legacy of sculptured stone is representative of the form that wood sculpture would have taken at the same period in time.

The passage of time has been divided historically into periods, and each period is associated with changes in tools, materials and design. Paleolithic or Old Stone Age man had the same instinctive creative desire that man has today, but the limitations imposed by his lack of knowledge and tools, meant that his sculpture was confined to his use of the natural shape or form of materials available, decorated by drawing or scratching on the surface of, for example, a stone or the protrusions on the cave wall.

Neanderthal man (*c.* 300,000 BC) provided us with an example of a bear's skeleton, arranged in a way which indicated to the archaeologists that it was perhaps a sporting trophy or maybe a god. Whatever its significance, it was nevertheless a sculptural composition. With the Mesolithic or Middle Stone Age (7000-5000 BC) period, there is evidence of progression in man's way of life. Man no longer needed to live in caves, he now had the knowledge and skill to build dwelling houses, and this new-found skill was also used to create new art forms.

Environmental changes brought about a change in animal distribution. The great roaming herds of animals decreased to be replaced by the lone forest animal, and man began to clear the forests for farming, reducing the need to hunt for his food. New tools were needed for this new way of life, such as the polished stone axe for clearing the forest, and the bow and arrow for hunting the lone animal. A new age was born – the Neolithic or New Stone Age (5000 BC).

It was Neolithic man who gave us the tools that we know today. Woodworking tools such as the axe, adze, burin, gouge and knife had cutting edges that were shaped from stone and bonded to their wooden handles with resin drawn from the birch tree. A comparison might be drawn between the high-speed steel and tungsten carbide tipped tools that we use today and the Neolithic wooden tools with stone tips. Our tools are made of steel and are often power driven, but the basic shape of the cutting edge has remained unchanged for some 3000 years. These tools were also used when manufacturing new forms of transport for Neolithic man. Canoes were carved from trunks of trees and the paddles carved and decorated. It was at this period that wood began to be carved to provide ornamentation as well as function. First came the tool, utensil or weapon, and then the decoration. It is interesting to note how weapons and tools were made into works of art. Bows, for instance, were carved at the hand position, and the handles of tools had surface decoration of carved animal heads.

Fear of the unknown caused man to devise gods that were worshipped for his protection. The representative form that these idols took was devised by the imagination of the sculptor. They were unconscious works of art based on the sculptor's tribal instincts and tradition. Works of art that have been handed down to us through the ages are expressions of the artist's thoughts or feelings and wood has been a sculptural medium for at least 5000 years. Even in places where timber is scarce, the roots of shrubs were used for ingenious figure carving with contorted root shapes giving emphasis to the sculptural form.

The earliest documented sculpture is that made in Egypt around 4000 BC with references in the Scriptures and inscriptions found in excavated tombs. Tutankhamun's tomb is an example which continues to amaze the world, together with sarcophagi which show that the ancient Egyptian had both the expertise and the technical knowledge to produce works of art with great qualities of endurance.

By 1300 BC, the mortice and tenon joint was in evidence, and dowels were often left to protrude as a decorative feature, being covered with gold leaf. Cedar was a wood favoured by Egyptian wood carvers. The tools used by the ancient Egyptians were made of iron, which was developed around the eighth century BC.

Egyptian-style sculpture gradually died out as other nations became dominant, but the Egyptian influence can be seen on early Greek sculptures. Wood was a preferred medium for the early Greeks but, unfortunately, nothing has survived. The ravages of time, together with the denunciation and destruction of idols by the early Christians have deprived posterity of so much sculpture in wood.

The Greeks later developed their own style, introducing a classical form which has never been surpassed. They thought of natural beauty as the greatest thing on earth and portrayed the natural form of the human figure, of animals and of plant life. The extent of Greek sculpture will never be known. Warlike tribes from Northern Greece destroyed much. The oldest specimens of Greek sculpture in existence are dated about 600 BC, but the 'classical age' is the late fifth century BC. The Romans continued the Greek interest in the naturalistically rendered human figure (second century BC – fourth century AD).

The early Christian period (AD 395-1000) gave us stone crosses, altars, goblets and plates. With the Romanesque period (AD 900-1100) came a resurgence of interest in sculpture, and elaborate decorations began to appear in churches. The Gothic style developed in France, Germany and England in the twelfth and thirteenth centuries. Craftsmen formed themselves into highly organised guilds and their statuary was part of the architecture. Small walnut and ivory carved statues of Christ and Mary are also a feature of this period.

From AD 1200, Italian sculpture began to develop new ideas and gradually to dominate the world of sculpture, with the centre of this new artistic movement at Florence. Nicola Pisano and his son Giovanni, Lorenzo Ghiberti, Donatello, Jacopo della Quercia and Michelangelo are among the most illustrious sculptors from this period, with the influence of Donatello in particular (1386-1466) lasting in Europe for many centuries. In fact his influence may be seen in the work of many present-day sculptors. He placed emphasis on expression – facial features were exaggerated to show the feelings of the subject, and the clothes were displayed in keeping with the character of the subject. Michelangelo (1475-1561) took this theme a stage further, with the human body becoming a prominent feature of gigantic works which have been marvelled at ever since. His talent and skill raised the status of the sculptor from that of an artisan to a creative artist. Michelangelo was also a painter and an architect.

In Britain, the Reformation of the sixteenth century saw the dissolution of the monasteries, and the resulting iconoclastic fervour caused the destruction of much of the early ecclesiastical works of art. The Elizabethans celebrated with great bonfires of images from our major cathedrals, and the Civil War of 1642–49 made the situation worse with zealous troops destroying almost everything. This was the Baroque period in Italy when geometric pattern played an important part in architecture. The Baroque influenced Grinling Gibbons who had been recommended to Sir Christopher Wren to carve the choir-stalls of the new St Paul's Cathedral. The genius of Grinling Gibbons produced the most intricate of wood carvings in the form of fruit and flowers, small animals and cherubs' heads, and Wren's design for the new cathedral made great play of this ability. During this period, much wood sculpture was gilded, the work being divided between the carpenters, who roughed out the design, and the carvers, who then carved the detail on the work, before passing it to the plasterers, painters and gilders for finishing. The specification in seventeenth-century contracts stated the type of wood to be used and finish required but, in addition, sought a guarantee from the artist that no cracks would appear in the finished work. The restoration of

Charles II to the English throne in 1660 halted much of the destruction of works of art, but the remaining antiquities were not fully appreciated. Even Christopher Wren authorised the destruction of imagery outside Westminster Abbey.

Modern sculpture draws its inspiration from many sources. Henri Matisse (1869–1954), painter and sculptor, was strongly influenced by Negro art. Other sculptors who have contributed originality to the techniques of wood sculpture in the twentieth century are Archipenko, Leon Underwood, Henry Moore and the Nigerian Ben Enwonwu, each of whom, in his own way, has developed styles and presentation that make his work unique. One fact remains clear, however, that through the ages, the beauty of nature's magnificence has always been absorbed instinctively and portrayed in shape and line or ornamentation. The tendency in modern sculpture is to emphasise the beauty of the grain pattern and natural form, whereas in the past gesso and paint hid the natural characteristics of the wood, although there is evidence in surviving examples to show that artists have always delighted in using natural form.

2 Wood Sculpture Related to Furniture

Wood carvers during the sixteenth and early seventeenth centuries in England began to use their skills to decorate domestic as well as ecclesiastical furniture. Heavy bulbous legs began to appear on farmhouse tables, with geometric incised carvings on the legs and apron. The same style of carving also appears on coffers, stools and boxes of this period, many of which were also dated. Most furniture of this period was made of oak.

The years during and after the English Civil War (1642-1649) were dominated by the Puritan influence. Furniture was plain, solid and functional. The sense of freedom generated by the restoration of Charles II in 1660 led to an increase of interest in furniture. Chairs in particular were highly decorated with 'barley sugar' twists forming the legs and back uprights, and intricately carved scrolls, cherubs' heads and crowns ornamenting the stretchers, arms and top rail. It was during this period that walnut (which was more easily carved than oak) first began to be used for furniture.

The eighteenth century is regarded as the high spot in English cabinet making, with the skills of the furniture maker and wood carver being used together to create some of the most beautiful and elegant furniture ever made. The early eighteenth century saw a move away from the exuberance of the Restoration period to a more restrained elegant style. Cabriole legs appeared on nearly every piece of furniture, often ornamented by acanthus leaves and ball and claw feet. The influence of William Kent during the 1730s and 1740s was revealed in very heavy solid decoration to furniture, a particular feature of his designs being tables with a very thick pedestal base decorated by dolphins. Mahogany from Cuba and Honduras was imported into England from the 1740s and its use gradually superseded the softer walnut of the previous century.

The mid eighteenth century was dominated by the influence of Thomas Chippendale, who is perhaps the most well known of all English cabinet makers. This was the time of the rococo period, with very light but extravagant decoration on houses, churches and furniture. Mirrors of this period were highly ornamented with scrolls, eagles and flowers. Asymmetric decoration was very popular. Chippendale was also influenced by the prevailing taste in the oriental, and 'Chinese Chippendale' became a recognised style, with the wood often decorated and carved to resemble bamboo and carved ivory. Even cottage furniture of this period was elegantly and accurately decorated, demonstrating the technical skill of the most humble carpenter.

Thomas Sheraton and George Hepplewhite were the main influences on late eighteenth-century furniture, which saw a return to the classical elegance of ancient Greece. The simple, elegant lines of reeding on the backs of chairs and the gentle tapering of the legs, combine to form a simple and understated design that has remained a classic style ever since.

The dawn of the nineteenth century saw the increasing development of the industrial revolution and a decline both in craftsmanship and, in the eyes of many, in design. The elegance of the late eighteenth century continued for a short while until the Regency period of 1810-20, when a change in style can be detected. There was a heavy Egyptian influence, which can be seen in the Brighton Pavilion built at this time. Striking black lacquer and gilt were used together on very heavy tables and chairs, together with boldly patterned veneers, the result being in some cases an eye-catching and elegant piece of furniture, and in others almost ugly.

As the century progressed, furniture became heavier and more solid, with the elegance and skill of the eighteenth-century craftsman becoming a thing of the past. The carvings decorating the backs of Victorian upholstered chairs, for example, although elaborate and sometimes beautifully executed, are more often than not shallower and less technically impressive than those of a hundred years earlier.

The Victorian Gothic period of the 1840s showed a return of interest in the mediaeval and Tudor styles, and many copies of sixteenth- and seventeenth-century chests and tables were produced, nearly all of which can be easily distinguished from the original by the same shallowness and lack of skill in the carving. It was at this period that wood staining became popular, with much of the beautiful natural grain being obscured by an opaque black lacquer.

The end of the nineteenth century saw a Sheraton revival, with a resurgence of interest in the elegance of the eighteenth century, often adapted to suit the Art Nouveau style, which had crept in with its stylised flowers and swirling shapes.

In the present century, very little carved decoration is seen on furniture, which is mainly in the plain clean lines of the modernistic style. However, the influence of the modern has furthered the development of sculpture for art's sake, with the emphasis being on abstract form.

Sculpture can be more appreciated when seen in its historical context. As much of European sculpture is set against a background of Christianity, mythology and history, so the art of other cultures must be seen as part of their heritage.

The stages in European history have certain parallels in other cultures but with differences in timing. For example, there is no evidence of the Iron Age ever taking place for the African bushman or pygmy; it appears that they had to wait for the missionaries of the nineteenth century. This parallel also applies to the North and South American Indians.

Tribal societies had their own customs and the rituals associated with these used wood to symbolise their beliefs. To refer to the art of these people as primitive gives entirely the wrong impression. Traditional art is a much better term and, when studied with the culture of the particular community, might be considered a sincere form of art. It represents beliefs which combine with the natural skill and imagination of the sculptor. Although it is difficult for one culture to relate to another, the development of sculpture is common to all. The sculptor is creating his impression of a subject. There may be constraints placed on him, such as not being able to carve a likeness for fear of being accused of witchcraft but, nevertheless, the end results have much in common and certain constraints exist for all sculpture.

II The Workshop

3 The Workshop or Studio

The sculptor's place of work may be anything from the kitchen table to the great outdoors. Small sculptures can easily be accommodated in the kitchen or a spare room in the house, whilst much of the work of Henry Moore, because of its size, has to be worked on outdoors. A craftsman's studio is a tool and as such needs to fit or suit the work. Consideration has to be given to location, size, shape etc. and, most importantly, has to be coupled with regard to the safety and comfort of the craftsman.

In the case of the kitchen or another room in the house, providing the wood chips and dust generated by the carving can be contained, there are few other problems. Wood chips are heavy and easily swept up; dust, however, is light and can be spread around the house by air currents. This can be avoided by keeping the doors shut and by not blowing on the work to clear the dust away after sanding. Equipment should be chosen with regard to the fact that the studio may have to double as a kitchen or a spare bedroom. This vice, for example (figure 1), may be easily clamped

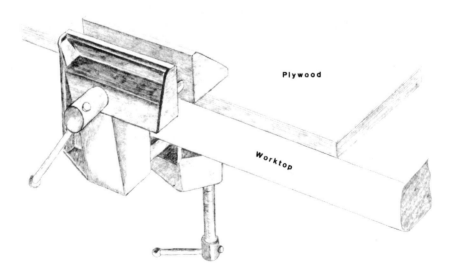

Plywood

Worktop

figure 1

to a table or worktop and is a very efficient holdfast. If a piece of 12mm (½in.) plywood, say 750mm (2ft 6in.) by 60mm (2½in.) is clamped between the vice and the worktop, protection is afforded and a space is provided for the tools.

The photograph in figure 2 shows the author's studio which is a weather-board timber framed and clad building. It has windows along the front (two of which may be opened) with the workbench running almost the entire length of the building directly under the windows. The interior is clad with insulation board. The door is situated at the end of the building to facilitate easy access for long lengths of timber. The windows face south for maximum light and are supplemented by a 1.5m (5ft) fluorescent natural daylight tube and an adjustable anglepoise lamp, fitted with a 100 watt bulb, clamped to the wall. Heating is provided by an electric convector heater with a thermostat control. This purpose-built studio is, however, suitable for small sculptures only. Larger work can be contained in the garage or garden shed. One famous sculptor even uses a polythene tent!

figure 2

In all studios, lighting is of paramount importance. Daylight is obviously best, but strong sunlight can be uncomfortable and make it difficult to see the finishing stage of the sculpture. If the sculptor is facing directly towards the sun, some form of shading, such as curtains or venetian blinds, is essential.

19

4 Safety in the Workshop

Safety in this context means consideration of the conditions required for producing good work. Good working conditions mean that the sculptor can relax in the knowledge that he has made every effort to provide for himself facilities which are both safe and comfortable. Safety can never be guaranteed, but many provisions can be made to avoid mistakes.

Before embarking on any job, questions have to be asked. Is there enough space for the work to be done? Is there sufficient light? Are the temperature and humidity suitable for both the sculptor and the timber he is using? Is there suitable storage space for the equipment and tools that will be used? Are there sufficient tools and materials for the job in hand? Above all else is the question 'Am I safe?'. Consider each question in turn. Space is important: there must be enough room to walk around without stumbling into something, and the bench must be large enough to lay the tools out on. If machines are sited in the workshop there must be enough space to operate them.

Lighting, by natural or artificial means, needs to be directed to provide the maximum benefit. If the sculptor cannot see what he is doing properly, mistakes and accidents can happen. Temperature and humidity have an effect on the timber used (see Chapter 10 for details), and they also have an effect on the craftsman and the tools that he uses. If the humidity is high the tools will rust and the sculptor might also be considered rusty if he languishes under high temperatures and humidity.

Sculptors working on large pieces of timber may not be able to choose their conditions of work, but it is important for them to consider the conditions imposed on them and at least make them safe. Working with very sharp tools is considered a dangerous practice at any time, but in very cold or wet conditions, the sensitivity that the sculptor needs in his hands may be lost, so it is essential that the craftsman wears gloves to protect them from the cold. A shelter of some sort may also be a necessity even if it is only an improvised polythene tent.

'A place for everything and everything in its place.' How many craftsmen can say that they find it easy to comply with the message in this old adage? The majority will undoubtedly have storage places for their tools which are used when the workshop is periodically cleaned and tidied, yet neglected when their minds are occupied with their work. It is not enough to provide storage for tools: discipline is needed to put the tools away after use. Much time will have been spent on sharpening woodcarving tools and to leave them on a cluttered bench is inviting trouble in two ways. The cutting edges are more likely to get damaged and there is also the danger that the sculptor himself might inadvertently cut himself on a partly concealed tool. Serious wood carvers will either have their tools laid out on the bench in a row, or placed in a canvas tool roll which both protects the edges of the tools and makes tool selection easier.

Removing a substantial amount of wood in the initial stages of carving creates many chips or shavings which seem to find their way into every nook and cranny. It is as well for the sculptor to discipline himself from the beginning to have regular cleaning sessions.

Using the wrong tool for the job can be risky. This may appear contrary to what is said in Chapter 7 about the improvisation of tools, but safety must come first, and if a safe tool cannot be improvised, then the correct tool must be obtained.

Using a penknife for carving wood is not recommended. Folding knives have a nasty habit of folding onto the fingers if the knife is not equipped with a lock to prevent this happening.

Blunt tools are the cause of many accidents. It takes far more force to make a blunt tool cut and, if the tool slips, this force is expended. If a hand or finger is in the way, the results can be imagined. Always hold a carving in one hand and the tool in the other, as this picture shows (figure 1), where the thumb acts as a counter to the pressure exerted. In other words, the thumb prevents the tool from slipping.

figure 1

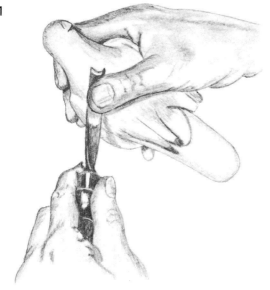

When a mallet is used with a carving tool, the force in the tool is commensurate with the blow but, when using the tool in the hands, one hand is required to push the tool and the other to guide, as will be seen in the diagram (figure 2 page 117) where two hands are being used to control light, paring cuts.

Dust is a problem to be countered, and an extraction system is warranted if machines are installed. Dust masks should be worn to prevent the inhalation of fine dust, and goggles or safety spectacles to protect the eyes from both the dust and the wood chips when rough carving.

Wedges used to secure the heads of hammers and some mallets must be tight, as should the handles of all tools, especially cutting tools. Woodcarving tools and files have pointed tangs which are a source of danger if the handles come off when using the tool.

When using knives, the rule of cutting away from the work should be followed whenever possible, using the thumb to exert

figure 2

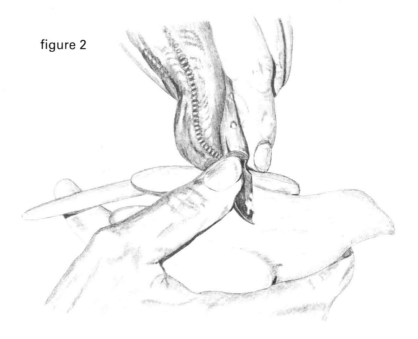

controlled pressure (figure 2). It is often necessary, however, to use the knife in the opposite direction and in this case a thumb guard of loose fitting leather should be worn (figure 3). A thumb cut from a leather gardening glove or industrial glove provides good protection. Sensitivity is lost if the thumb guard is too tight.

Breaking glass for use as scrapers should be carried out between sheets of paper or cloth to prevent the glass from flying. Care should also be exercised when using the glass, and it is well worth wrapping a piece of masking tape around the edge that is held in the hand.

figure 3

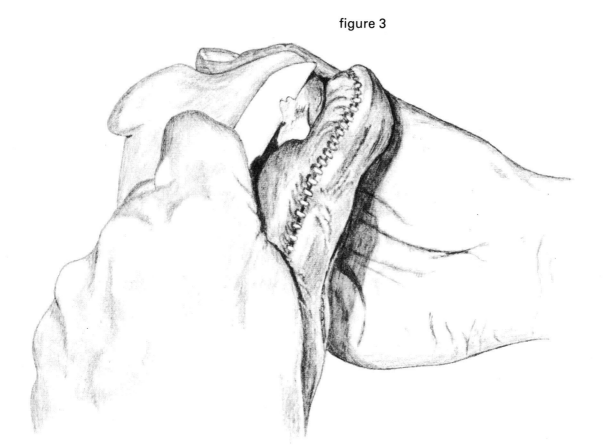

FLAMMABLE LIQUIDS

Many kinds of solvents accumulate in a workshop – polishes, thinners, methylated spirit etc. Old rusty tins should be discarded and only the quantity of solvent that is in use should be kept. Solvents must be stored in marked containers well away from the heating source and in accordance with the manufacturer's recommendations.

Grindstones running eccentrically at high speed are a danger. If the load on the wheel is out of balance, the wheel could burst. With all grinding machines, a device for truing the wheel is a necessity.

Electrical safety must never be taken for granted. The correct fuse for the power rating of the tool should be fitted. Periodic checks on the earthing should also be carried out, and trailing leads avoided. Working with power tools in wet conditions is not a wise thing to do and, if it is proposed to use such tools out of doors, an earth leakage circuit breaker should be fitted.

Keeping floors clear of obstacles, putting things away after use and cleaning up the mess made are the attributes of an efficient craftsman.

5 Tools

It is with some trepidation that the reader is introduced to the subject of tools. The number of tools described, which may appear formidable, are those used to execute the types of work discussed in this book, but it will be seen that the tool requirements for any single project are quite small.

The market in tools has always been a competitive one and, with this in mind, purchasing a quality tool is of paramount importance. Steel cutting tools are only as good as the composition of the metal coupled with the craftsmanship used in their manufacture. A long lasting cutting edge is important, not only because less time is spent in sharpening the tool, but it is also much safer to use a sharp tool than a blunt one. So, when buying any tool get the best possible, even though the quality is reflected in its price.

This introduction to wood carving endeavours to explain the way the various tools may be used. There is a vast number to choose from and an understanding of their usage will help the reader make a selection. The tools referred to in this book have been selected from a study of British and American catalogues and the list is by no means comprehensive. It is hoped that sufficient information is provided for the prospective sculptor to select the tool he requires without too much difficulty and, if he has to order by post, to feel confident that his choice is the correct one.

WOODCARVING TOOLS

The basic tools of the wood sculptor are the chisels and gouges that help him form the contours of his work. Often these tools are supplied without handles, thereby enabling the wood carver to obtain both the tool and the handle which suit him personally. The purchaser has the choice of fitting the handle himself or asking the supplier to fit it for him. Some tools come fitted with attractively polished handles whilst others again are presented as boxed sets. Although these boxed sets make good presents, experience will show that the best method of building up a set of tools is to purchase the tool required at the time it is needed, preferably by personal inspection.

Chisels

To explain the function of the chisel, a comparison is made between the firmer chisel that the carpenter or cabinet maker uses, and the chisel of the wood carver.

The firmer chisel has a flat surface on one side because the joints that the carpenter makes for his constructions all have flat sides, as will be seen in this diagram (figure 1) of a tenon joint being cut. To use a woodcarving chisel on this same job would have obvious disadvantages, since this tool does not have a flat face to guide it, and therefore has a tendency to dig into the wood. A curved surface

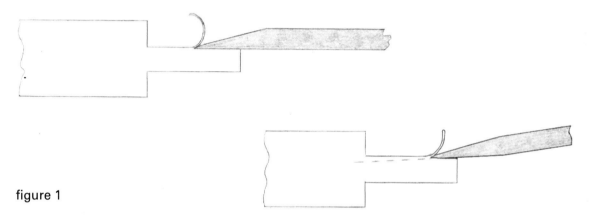

figure 1

presented to the firmer means that the bevelled side has to make contact with the work to cut the curve, whereas the bent woodcarving chisel has been purposely shaped for such profiles (figure 2). Chisels are used where the carved surfaces are either

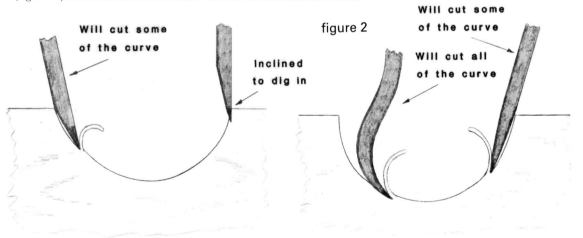

Will cut some of the curve

Inclined to dig in

figure 2

Will cut some of the curve

Will cut all of the curve

Firmer chisel

Bent chisel and straight chisel

figure 3

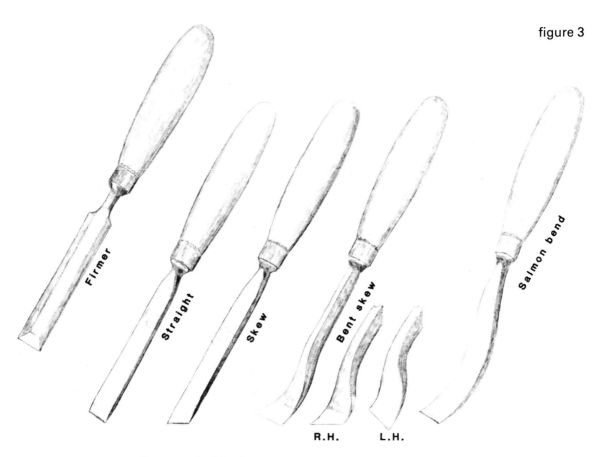

Firmer

Straight

Skew

Bent skew

R.H.   L.H.

Salmon bend

Types of chisel

rounded, flat or a combination of both. The fact that it has a curved bevel on each side allows greater freedom for the tool to follow the contours of the sculpture. Figure 3 shows the types of chisel available.

Size (width of cutting edge) of chisels that are usually available.

Straight Chisels

Size									
(mm)	3	5	6	10	12	16	18	25	32
(in.)	⅛	³⁄₁₆	¼	⅜	½	⅝	¾	1	1¼

Bent Chisels

Size									
(mm)	2	3	5	6	8	10	12	16	18	25
(in.)	¹⁄₁₆	⅛	³⁄₁₆	¼	⁵⁄₁₆	⅜	½	⅝	¾	1

Salmon Bend Chisels
Size

(mm)	2	6	10	12
(in.)	$1/16$	$1/4$	$3/8$	$1/2$

Skew Chisels
Size

(mm)	2	3	5	6	10	12	16	18	25	32
(in.)	$1/16$	$1/8$	$3/16$	$1/4$	$3/8$	$1/2$	$5/8$	$3/4$	1	$1\,1/4$

Bent Skew Chisels RH or LH
Size

(mm)	2	3	5	6	8	10	12	16	18	25
(in.)	$1/16$	$1/8$	$3/16$	$1/4$	$5/16$	$3/8$	$1/2$	$5/8$	$3/4$	1

Accessibility is the reason for the shapes of these tools. The bent tools deal with differing degrees of curvature, whilst the skew chisels are for working into sharp corners or for producing a slicing cut, which is often an advantage when finishing.

figure 4

Gouges

The gouge is the tool most frequently used by the carver. It is used in both the roughing and finishing stages. Before confusing the reader with the permutations involved in the choice of these tools, it would be as well to consider its use.

Consider the cutting edge of a shallow gouge as compared with that of a no. 9 gouge (figure 4). Although both tools are the same width, the depth of cut that each tool is capable of is very different. The no. 9 gouge would therefore be the tool chosen for making the heavy cuts necessary when roughing out because it removes a greater volume of wood with each cut.

The curvature, usually referred to as the sweep, of the cutting edge is also designed to fit the curvature of the surface being worked on. The criteria for the choice of gouge are its type, size and sweep as related to the form being worked on.

Figure 5 shows the types of gouge, and also the shape or profile of the cutting edge of each tool. This sweep of the tool is given a number, the lower the number indicating the larger the radius of the tool.

No.10
No.8
No.6
No.4

No.11
No.9
No.7
No.5
No.3

Sweep(or shape)of cut the gouge makes

Size (width of cutting edge) of gouges that are usually available.

Straight Gouges
Sweep No. 3, 5, 6, 7, 9

Size								
(mm)	3	5	6	10	12	16	18	25
(in.)	1/8	3/16	1/4	3/8	1/2	5/8	3/4	1

Bent Gouges (Front and Back Bent)
Sweep No. 4, 8, 10, 11

Size							
(mm)	2	3	5	6	10	12	16	18
(in.)	1/16	1/8	3/16	1/4	3/8	1/2	5/8	3/4

Salmon Bend Gouges
Sweep No. 3, 4, 6, 7, 8, 9

Size							
(mm)	2	3	5	6	10	12	16	18
(in.)	1/16	1/8	3/16	1/4	3/8	1/2	5/8	3/4

figure 5

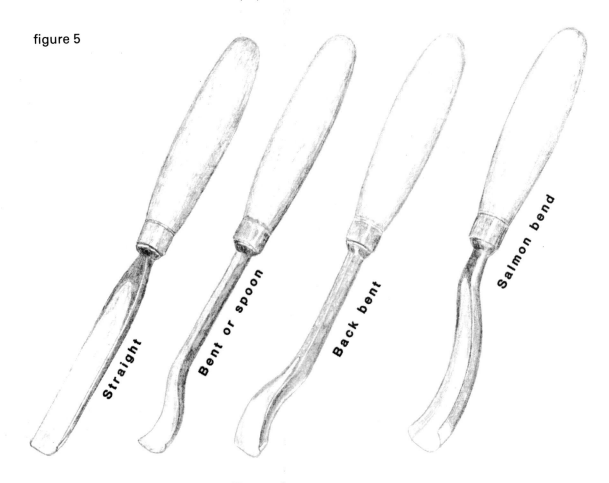

Straight   Bent or spoon   Back bent   Salmon bend

Types of gouge

The study of tool catalogues will show that different manufacturers have their own systems for designating tool selection. Where one major supplier has a numbering system which signifies the type and shape of all their tools, another has a numbering system from one to eleven (which is common to all gouge sweeps), coupled with a word description of type and size. For example, a no. 19 to the first supplier denotes a salmon bend gouge with a 10 sweep, whereas if a similar tool was bought from another supplier, he would specify it as a no. 10 salmon bend. All this means that selection of tools requires careful study of the catalogues.

While on the subject of gouges, there are two that deserve special consideration. The no. 10 gouge is sometimes referred to as a fluter, the no. 11 gouge is known as a veiner and, as their names imply, the traditional use of these tools was in cutting semi-cylindrical grooves in pillars and veins in foliage. Because the cutting edges of both these tools extend beyond a semi-circle, their cutting action is slightly different to that of other gouges. It may be thought that the veiner is the best tool for roughing out a carving but in actual fact this is not so; because it cuts such a deep channel it is difficult to visualise the new surface. Also, when using the larger size veiners, the tendency is not to cut to the full depth of the tool because it requires more effort, and when this happens it has a decided disadvantage. A shallower gouge will remove stock with far less effort. One advantage shared by both the fluter and the veiner is their ability to double as both gouge and chisel.

In a situation such as that shown in this diagram (figure 6), where an undercut is required in a sculpture, the shape can be achieved simply by rolling the tool over to a different angle and using the side of the cutting edge.

figure 6

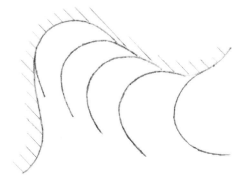

Using the side of the cutting edge as a shallow gouge or chisel

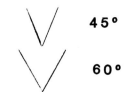

45°

60°

90°

Some of the angles available

Parting Tools or Vee Tools

These tools are used for undercutting and lining in such as marking shallow grooves to denote the outline of a relief carving. They are difficult to sharpen, as will be seen in Chapter 6, and therefore need more care. Incised carving is probably the function where this tool comes into its own. If the form required is correct for the tool available, the speed of execution of the work is far greater than if the vee shaped groove was cut with other tools. Figure 7 shows the types of parting tools available.

figure 7

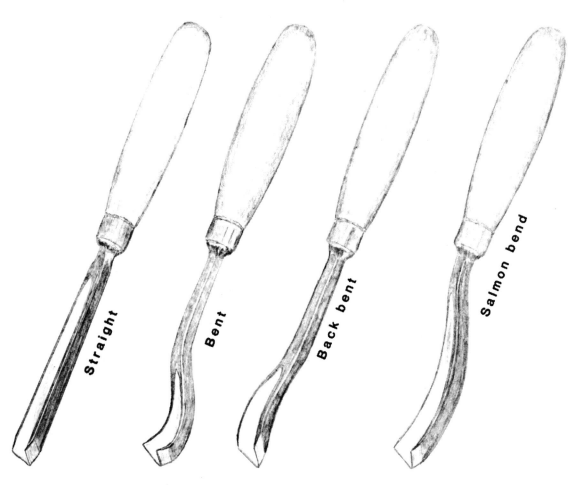

Straight

Bent

Back bent

Salmon bend

Types of parting tool

Size (width of cutting edge) of parting tools that are usually available.

Straight Parting Tools
Angle 45°, 60°, 90°

Size					
(mm)	3	5	6	10	12	16
(in.)	⅛	³⁄₁₆	¼	⅜	½	⅝

Bent Parting Tools (Front and Back Bent)
Angle 45°, 60°, 90°

Size					
(mm)	3	5	6	10	12	16
(in.)	⅛	³⁄₁₆	¼	⅜	½	⅝

Salmon Bend Parting Tools
Angle 45°, 60°, 90°

Size			
(mm)	3	6	10	12
(in.)	⅛	³⁄₁₆	⅜	½

Macaroni and Fluteroni
These tools for the purpose of this book might be considered special tools. Like all tools they have been designed for a purpose and their purchase requires justification. To explain this, the shape of the parting tool is considered alongside that of a macaroni (figure 8).

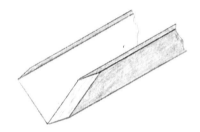 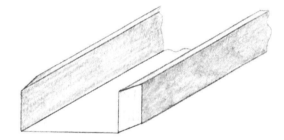

Parting tool   **Macaroni**   figure 8

A channel in the macaroni form can be achieved by using a parting tool to cut the sides (figure 9) and a chisel to cut out the bottom. (If the channel is a long one, a bent chisel may be required.) If many such channels are required, however, the proper shaped tool would be a decided advantage. If the channel to be cut has a small radius in the corners, then the sides would be cut with a veiner or, if justified, the correct tool would be a fluteroni (figure 9).

The wood carver will come across other strange sounding terms applied to carving tools such as fish tail, alongee etc., but most of these are special purpose tools and as it is assumed that an enthusiastic carver will be getting a catalogue of tools, their description here would only serve to confuse.

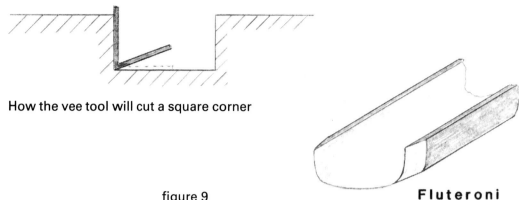

How the vee tool will cut a square corner

figure 9

Fluteroni

Fitting Handles to Woodcarving Tools

The end of the tool which receives the handle is of a tapered square section and the corners of the square are sharp enough to cut and behave as a reamer. Holding the tool in the jaws of the vice with some padding to protect the tool (figure 10), the handle (which is supplied pre-drilled) is pushed on and turned at the same time. This cuts a tapered hole which extends until the end of the handle is about 6mm ($\frac{1}{4}$in.) from the end of the taper. The handle is then gently tapped on until it touches the metal shoulder.

figure 10

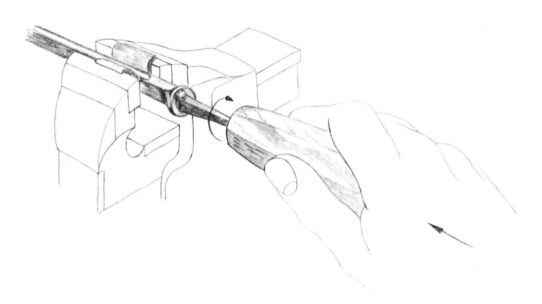

Diameter of holes to be drilled

32

Another method is to drill two holes in the handle which will allow it to accommodate the taper, as the diagram shows, and then tap it on with a mallet. The diameter of the holes may be taken as the diagonal at approximately one third points along the taper.

CARVING KNIVES

The knives shown in figure 11 have been chosen from a number of catalogues as the types most useful to the sculptor. The penknife is also illustrated, but as a warning. Folding knives are acceptable to the serious carver *only* if the blade is locked. A sharp knife folding on to the fingers holding the carving can cause a nasty accident.

Chip carving is explained in a later chapter and it is this type of

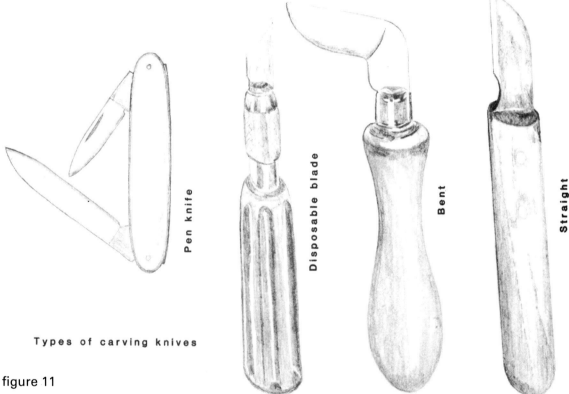

Types of carving knives

figure 11

work, together with whittling, which is associated with carving knives, but they nevertheless have a definite use in all types of carving and a selection of knives is well worth having.

A carving will sometimes present a problem which can most easily be overcome with a knife. For instance, if the subject is of an awkward shape which has to be held in the hand, it may well be difficult to use the normal carving tools. Every carving tool requires guidance and restraint and, if this cannot be provided, the knife might be the answer. Perhaps this can best be illustrated by peeling an apple with a knife. The apple is held in one hand whilst the knife is held in the other and the thumb of this hand acts as both guide and restraint. Imagine trying to peel the same apple with a chisel!

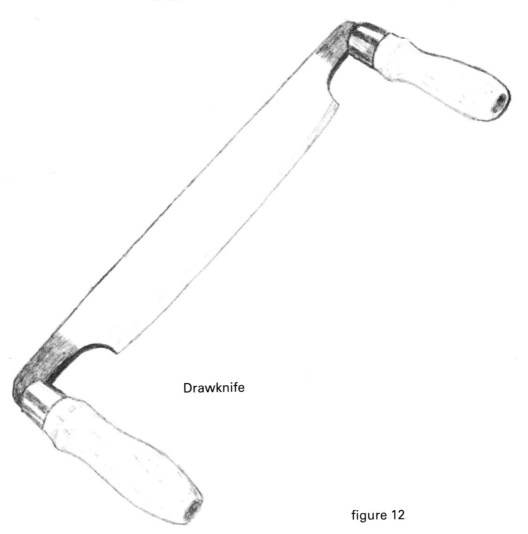

Drawknife

figure 12

DRAWKNIFE (figure 12)

This is a most useful tool for working with the grain of the wood to remove stock quickly and easily. The workpiece must be held firmly and the tool is used by gripping the handles and drawing it towards you. This tool is used extensively in rural crafts such as trug making (figure 13), and the sculptor finds it a boon when working on long sweeping curves. It is essentially a tool for roughing out, as far as its use in wood sculpture is concerned.

34

figure 13

SPOKESHAVE (figure 14)
As its name implies, the shaping of spokes of a wheel may have
been the original use for this tool, but it is used by most
woodworking crafts where curved surfaces have to be cut. The
sculptor of abstract forms which require a smooth finish has an
ideal tool in the spokeshave. When set to take a fine cut, the finish
it produces is similar to that produced on a flat surface by a
smoothing plane.

figure 14

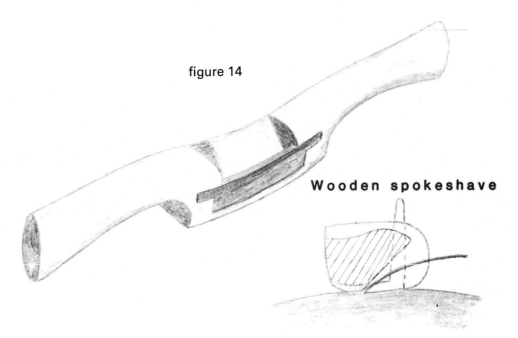

Wooden spokeshave

Sectioned to show how it cuts

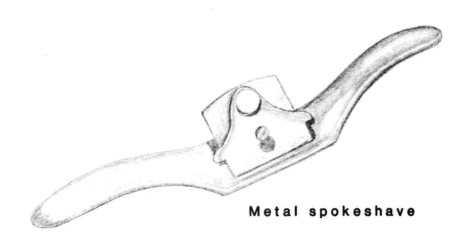

Metal spokeshave

RASPS AND RIFFLERS

Rasps and rifflers are hardened metal strips with raised teeth, similar to engineer's files, used for the controlled shaping of a workpiece that has been roughly carved. These tools will not give a smooth finish, but their ability to shape a surface makes them a useful addition to the tool kit. A few examples of rasps and rifflers are shown in this diagram (figure 15). There are other shapes and lengths available.

figure 15

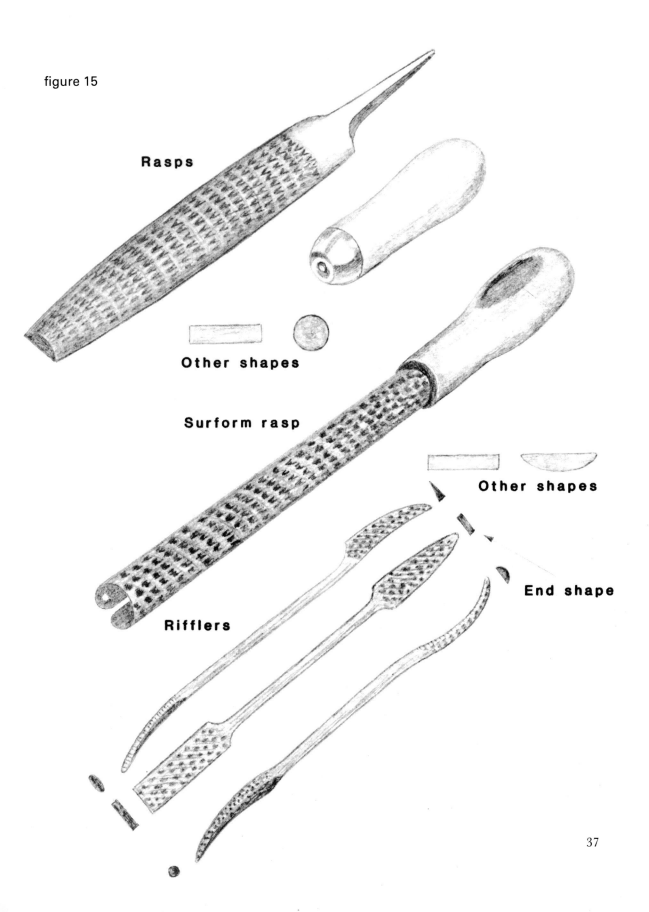

Rasps

Other shapes

Surform rasp

Other shapes

End shape

Rifflers

37

SCRAPERS

Scrapers are used to scrape the surface of a sculpture, to remove or reduce the marks from abrasive paper and to speed up the sanding operation. They are thin plates of carbon steel which have their edges sharpened in a way that allows the tool to cut a very fine shaving. Often they are made by the craftsman himself from old circular saw blades, or purchased as cabinet scrapers and re-shaped as in figure 16. Broken glass is also sometimes used as a scraper and the whittler will use his knife.

figure 16

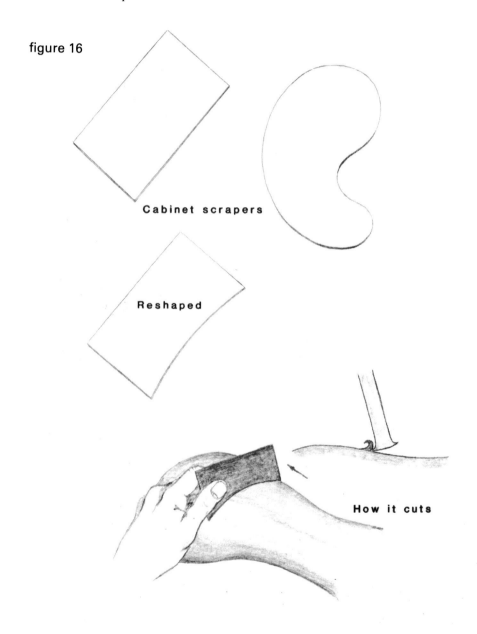

Cabinet scrapers

Reshaped

How it cuts

SAWS

Hand saws (figure 17)

Saws cut away the waste wood and are a most important part of the wood sculptor's tool kit. He requires a rip saw for cutting longitudinally or with the grain, and a cross cut saw for cutting across the grain.

figure 17

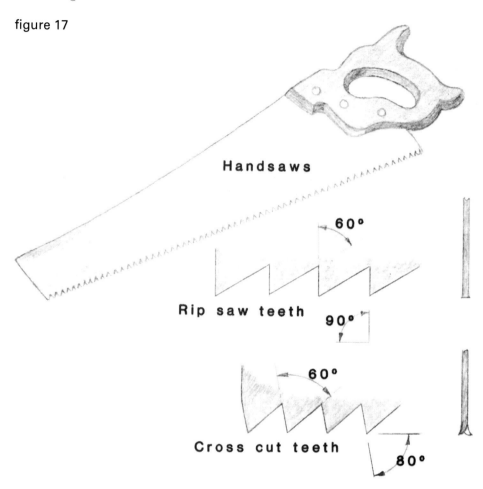

Handsaws

60°

Rip saw teeth

90°

60°

Cross cut teeth

80°

Rip saws have teeth that number four to every 25mm (1in.) of length. The rip saw cuts through the fibres of the wood and for this the teeth are sharpened straight across (figure 18).

Cross cut saws have teeth that number from eight to ten for every 25mm (1in.) of length and they depend on the set of the teeth to give clearance to the saw while cutting. Figure 18 shows the design of the teeth for their function, which is to cut through the fibres and, at the same time, to push them outwards.

Bow or chair saws are designed for cutting profiles and, in the

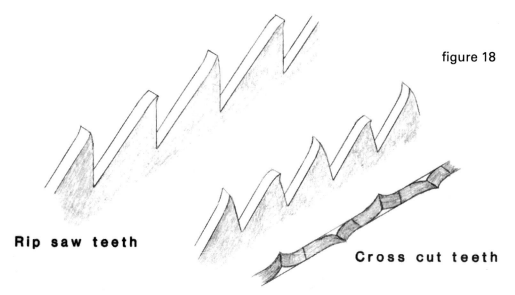

Rip saw teeth

Cross cut teeth

figure 18

absence of a band saw, may be considered essential if a lot of roughing out is to be avoided (figure 19).

As the band saw has been mentioned, it would be as well to say that, because most of the wood the sculptor uses is of large section, the depth of cut of such a saw also needs to be large. This makes it a very expensive piece of machinery.

figure 19

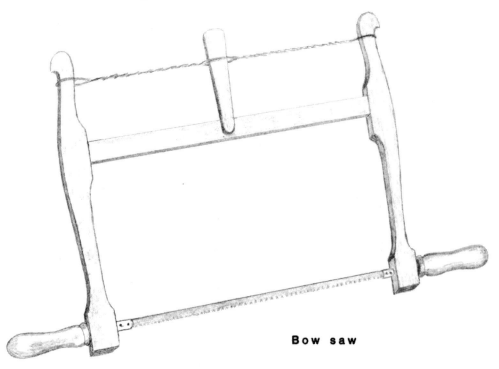

Bow saw

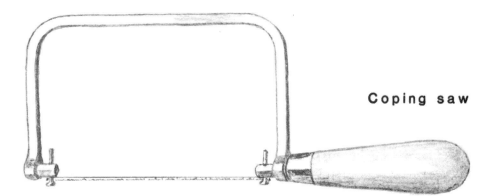

Coping saw

figure 20

Coping saws are like a small version of the bow saw. Their teeth are quite fine making them the ideal tool for profiling small work (figure 20).

Chain saws

This photograph (figure 21) illustrates an example of chain saw carving where the techniques of the forester have been used for both roughing out and detailing a carving which stands about 2m (6ft 6in.) high. Power tools create a branch of wood carving entirely separate from traditional craftsmanship, and would be a departure from the text of this book.

figure 21

DIVIDERS

Dividers are used for checking on symmetry and for taking measurements from a drawing for comparison with the sculpture. The proportional dividers serve the same purpose, but have the added advantage of being able to scale up or down (figure 22).

figure 22

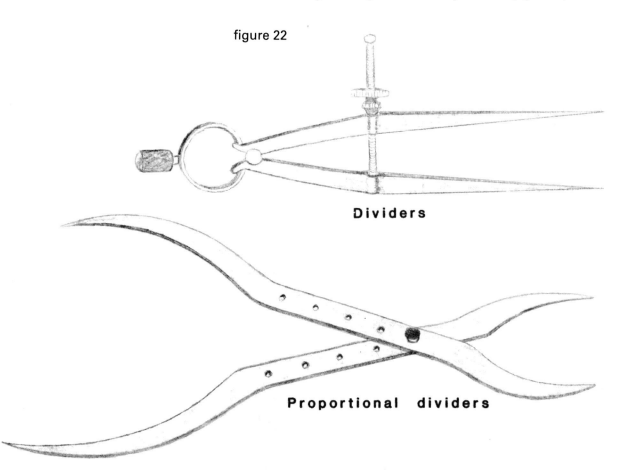

Dividers

Proportional dividers

HOLDFASTS

Sculpture that is not sufficiently heavy and stable enough to support itself requires a holdfast or clamp to hold it securely and, at the same time, allow the sculptor access to as much of the work as possible. The type of holdfast used will depend on the size of the timber and the way in which it is to be worked. For instance, if a slab of wood is to be used for a relief or incised carving, it may simply be clamped to the bench, whereas if it is a carving in the round other ways have to be found.

More often than not the bench will be the supporting piece and the work will be secured to it. It may be a vice or some other type of clamping device which holds the work firmly to the bench itself. Whichever way the timber is held the bench must be rigid, and if a free standing bench is used it must be robustly made and heavy. Figure 23 illustrates a free standing bench, and the sizes given are suitable for a sitting position but an alternative height is given for the carver who has to stand. Mortice and tenon joints are suggested for the construction of the frame and the timber may be whatever is available, but beech or a similar dense hardwood is recommended for the top. A shelf across the lower rails will, if loaded with a heavy tool box or piece of stone, increase the rigidity.

figure 23

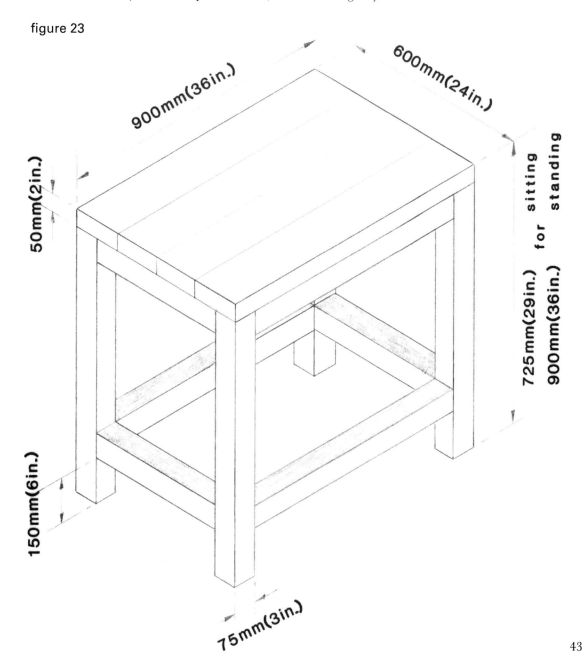

VICES

The vice is a matter of choice and depends to a certain extent on the type of work to be carried out.

An engineer's vice is preferred by many serious wood carvers (figure 24). This has the advantage of providing an extremely positive grip, since the mass increases rigidity, but there is a possible disadvantage of crushing the work if the jaws are tightened too much.

A carpenter's vice (figure 25) is the most generally useful for the woodworker and, when the jaws have been lined with wood or felt, protection is provided for the workpiece. A possible disadvantage is the height of the vice from the ground when working on small sculptures.

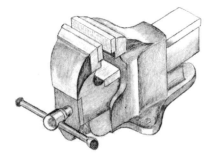

figure 24

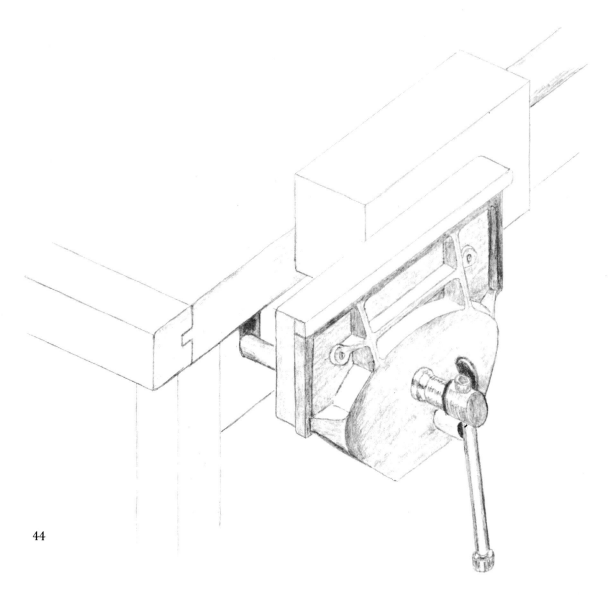

figure 25

The wood carver's vice, or *Scopas Chops* (figure 26) as it is usually called, is a versatile tool which may be fixed permanently to the bench or used as a portable holdfast, either clamped to the bench or held in the bench vice.

Whatever vice is chosen by the sculptor, it is useful for him to have a small engineer's vice in some readily available spot for the odd metal working job which has to be accommodated.

CLAMPS

Clamps are a useful addition and a tool that the woodworker never has enough of. Their prime function is to apply pressure when work is being glued up, but they have other uses and may be considered as a third hand for holding work. The type of clamp used is dependent on the extent of the pressure required together with the capacity required. Figure 27 shows a few of the types of clamps available with the 'G' or 'C' clamp being the most used general purpose clamp. The sash clamp was a tool designed for clamping window sashes, door frames and so on, but it has other uses, as the schematic diagram shows (figure 28). (Clamps are often referred to as cramps, and their function is clamping or cramping. To avoid confusion, the words clamp and clamping are used throughout this book.)

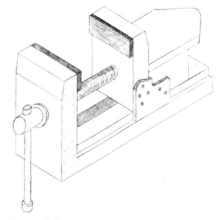

figure 26

figure 27

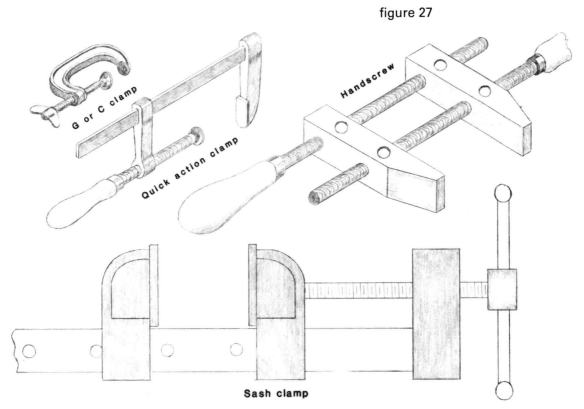

G or C clamp

Quick action clamp

Handscrew

Sash clamp

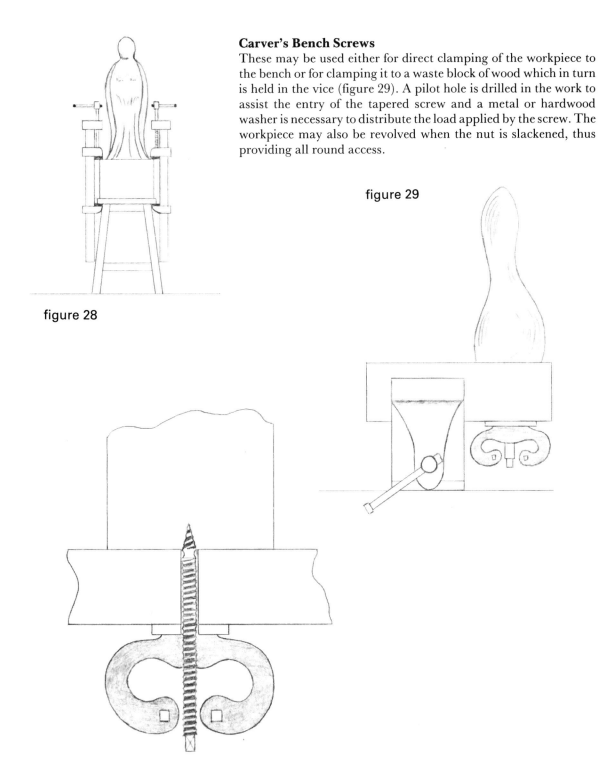

Carver's Bench Screws

These may be used either for direct clamping of the workpiece to the bench or for clamping it to a waste block of wood which in turn is held in the vice (figure 29). A pilot hole is drilled in the work to assist the entry of the tapered screw and a metal or hardwood washer is necessary to distribute the load applied by the screw. The workpiece may also be revolved when the nut is slackened, thus providing all round access.

figure 29

figure 28

6 Maintenance of Tools

The care of tools is very important, not least because neglected tools can be dangerous. Tools that function well are a pleasure to use but the opposite is the case when tools do not perform as they should. Tempers get frayed and chances are taken which are reflected in the work.

Sharpening woodcarving tools can be a frustrating task to the inexperienced. A sharp-edged tool is essential for all carving techniques, and practice and understanding are needed to obtain this sharp edge.

SHARPENING STONES

Both natural and artificial abrasive stones are available and so, whilst the selection of sharpening stones will be a matter for personal preference, a few remarks on the characteristics of various stones may help in making a choice.

Natural Stones
The Washita is the fastest cutting of the natural stones and is used for the initial sharpening.

Soft Arkansas is another fast-cutting natural stone that is recommended for general sharpening. It provides a good cutting edge which may be further improved with a hard Arkansas stone.

Hard Arkansas is a very hard natural stone used to impart the final edge only.

Welsh Slate is another stone recommended for obtaining a fine cutting edge quickly.

Artificial Stones
These are made from silicone carbide and aluminium oxide, graded as coarse, medium and fine. Cutting principles of sharpening stones are the blunting and wearing away of abrasive particles to expose fresh particles. The artificial stone particles are embedded in a matrix which allows the release of blunt particles.

Both types of stone are supplied in a variety of shapes and sizes (figure 1).

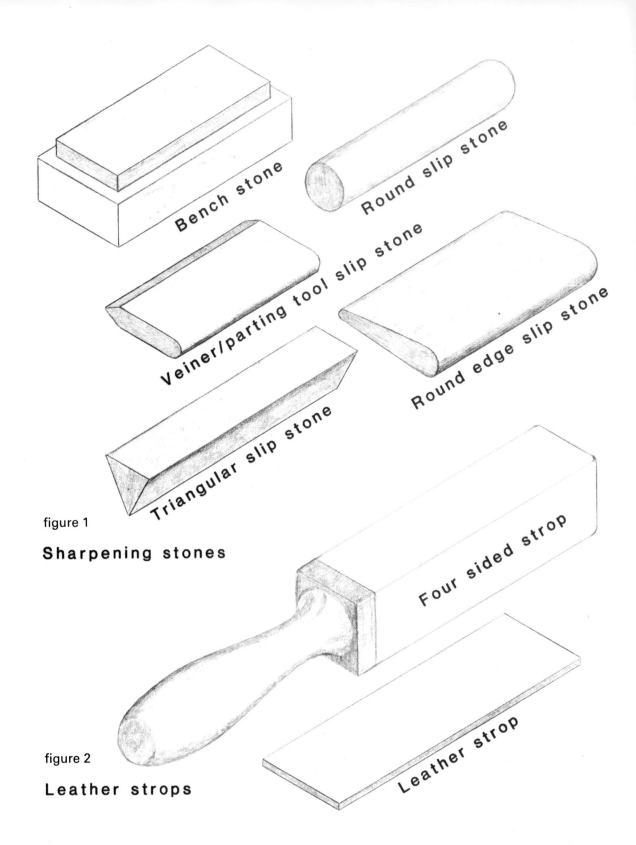

Bench stone

Round slip stone

Veiner/parting tool slip stone

Round edge slip stone

Triangular slip stone

figure 1

Sharpening stones

Four sided strop

Leather strop

figure 2

Leather strops

Bench Stones are rectangular blocks which the sculptor uses for sharpening chisels, the outside bevels of gouges and other edged tools. Sizes are usually 200mm (8in.) x 50mm (2in.) or 150mm (6in.) x 50mm (2in.).

Slip Stones are made to accommodate the shapes of the tool. Round edge slips are used for sharpening the inside bevel of gouges and the curvature of this should closely approximate the curvature of the tool for maximum efficiency. Knife edge or triangular slips are for sharpening the inside bevel of parting tools.

STROPS (figure 2)

These are strips of leather which have the effect of polishing the edge of the tool to a high degree of sharpness. For the ultimate in sharpness, two strops are required, one of which has been dressed with crocus powder and the other left untreated. (Crocus is a very fine abrasive powder and, when mixed with a vegetable oil, makes a strop dressing which also keeps the leather soft and pliable.)

It is a decided advantage to strop tools frequently to maintain the keen cutting edge. It takes so little time that it is worth having the strops in a permanent handy position.

SHARPENING OF WOODCARVING TOOLS

When sharpening woodcarving tools, two angles have to be considered: the grinding angle and the honing angle. The grinding angle is that produced by the tool manufacturer and is usually in the region of 15°. The honing angle is produced by the craftsman and is usually about 20° (figure 3).

figure 3

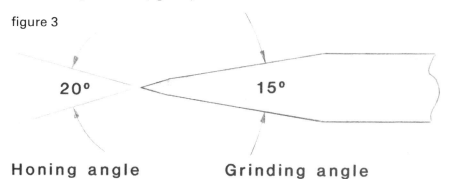

Honing angle   Grinding angle

The cutting angle of the tool used will depend on the hardness of the timber being cut. Soft woods respond well to very sharp edged acute-angled tools, but if a sharp-angled tool is used on hard woods, the thin cutting edge is liable to break under the strain. Perhaps the rule should be that if the wood is soft enough to pare easily using hand pressure and not the mallet, then an acute-edged tool may be used, but if the mallet is required, then stick close to the 20° angle.

New tools are often supplied ground to shape only. It is then up

to the craftsman to give them a good cutting edge. This diagram
(figure 4) shows how a new gouge looks when held up to the light.
The narrow band of reflected light at the end of the tool shows how
much metal has to be worn away in the sharpening process in order
to obtain a keen cutting edge.

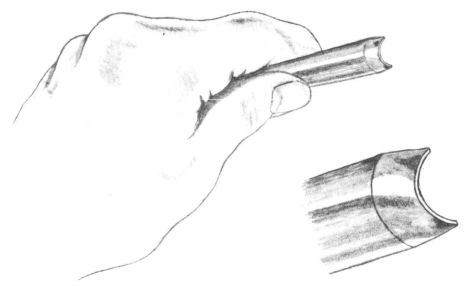

figure 4

Sharpening Chisels

Chisels are probably the most straightforward of all the edge tools
to sharpen, and they require that the ground edge of the tool be
examined to determine the extent of any uneven grinding. This
shows as an uneven band of light and indicates where more
pressure is required when honing to produce an even cutting edge.
To turn the ground edge of the tool into a good cutting edge, the
coarse or medium bench stone is used (figure 5).

After wetting the stone with oil, the ground face of the tool is held
against it (A) to establish the grinding angle. The back of the tool
is then raised by a degree or so (B) and the tool pushed to and fro.
Keep it at a constant angle and with a slight downward pressure of
the hand holding the front of the tool against the stone.

The metal will be gradually worn away and, when the excess oil
is wiped off, the cutting edge will then be revealed as a shiny line
when the tool is held to the light (figure 6 A). The tool is then
turned over and the process repeated until the two 'shiny lines'
meet to form the cutting edge. Where these two edges meet, a burr
or rough edge of metal (B) will be formed and can be felt when the
thumb is passed down the tool (C). The roughness of this burr will

figure 5

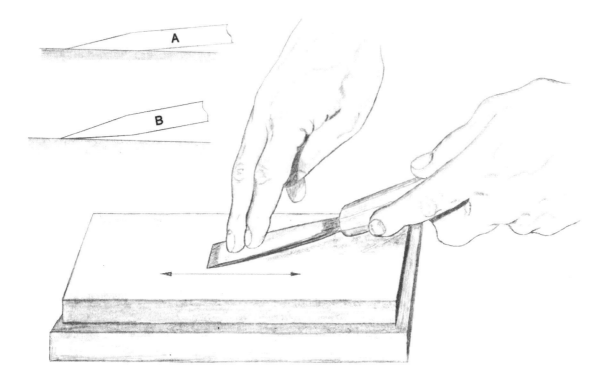

figure 6

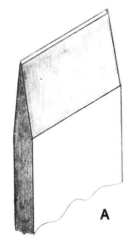

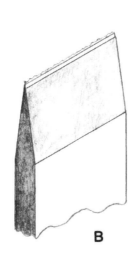

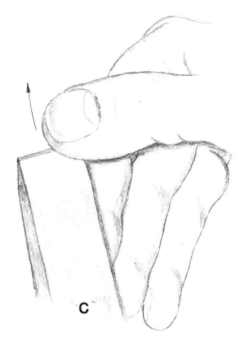

vary according to the grade of sharpening stone used. A coarse stone produces a rough edge, whereas the edge produced by a very fine stone can hardly be detected.

The tool is honed against a fine carborundum or soft Arkansas stone in exactly the same way as the previous stone, checking the sharpness from time to time. Expensive natural stones such as Arkansas and Washita may induce the expediency of using a slip stone mounted in a wooden tray for use as a bench stone. The tray could be simply a piece of wood recessed to house the stone and held in the vice (figure 7 A).

A check for sharpness which also helps to remove the 'wire edge' or burr is actually to cut some wood. Hold a piece of wood in the vice and cut across the grain at a slight angle to produce a slicing cut (B). If the tool cuts reasonably well, a few more rubs on the fine

figure 7

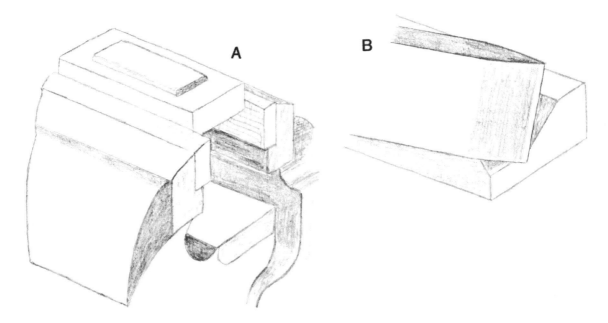

A

B

stone will prepare it for the leather strop (figure 8), which should be prepared or dressed with crocus powder and a lubricant such as tallow or neatsfoot oil. The tool is held in a similar manner to that used when using the sharpening stone, but now the strokes should be made in one direction only, that is away from the cutting edge. If desired, the strop could be fixed to a flat strip of wood, although it works equally well laid on a flat bench. After a few passes over the strop, the tool is ready for use. Leather strops should be kept clean and stored in a polythene bag, which has the added advantage of preventing the strop from drying out.

52

figure 8

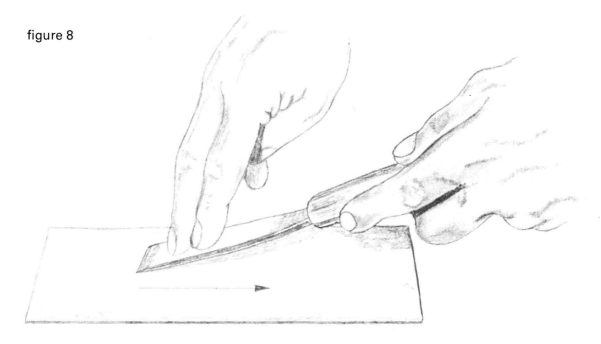

Sharpening Small Carving Tools

When narrow tools have to be sharpened, it can be difficult to hold them at the correct angle. The small size makes the craftsman insensitive to the bearing of the tool which results in uneven sharpening.

The sensitivity lost by taking the tool to the stone can be somewhat overcome by taking the stone to the tool. This has the advantage that it is much easier to feel the angle at which the tool is to be held, but care must be taken to prevent the hand coming into contact with the cutting edge, should the stone slip off the tool (figure 9).

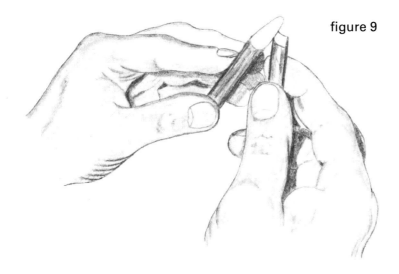

figure 9

Sharpening Gouges

Gouges are sharpened in a similar way to chisels, but the sweep of the cutting edge, however, necessitates the tool being rotated while being rubbed on the stone (figure 10). The expert will use a figure of eight pattern for the tool's journey around the bench stone to ensure that the wear on the stone is even. The less experienced may traverse the tool along the length of the stone, moving forward to regulate the wear on the stone and then back again.

figure 10

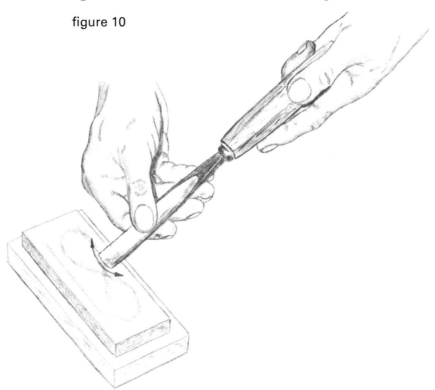

Sharpening the inside of the gouge is the work of the slipstone (figure 11) and involves removing the burr formed when rubbing the outside edge on the bench stone. First the stone is rubbed along the groove (A) and then the back of the stone should be raised a few degrees to form the inside cutting edge (B). This reduces the burr and pushes what remains to the outside edge, where it is removed on the bench stone using a finer cutting stone than that used previously. When the craftsman is satisfied that the burr has been completely removed and the tool is sharp, the outside edge is then stropped. The tool is drawn in one direction only, away from the cutting edge, to avoid cutting the leather and is simultaneously rotated. The inside edge is stropped by folding the leather and pressing it into the groove of the tool whilst drawing it towards the cutting edge (figure 12).

figure 11

figure 12

Sharpening the Parting Tool

The parting tool (figure 13) is undoubtedly the most difficult of all tools to sharpen. It is shaped like two chisels meeting to form one tool (A) but, because the junction between the two tool shapes has a small radius, the outside form of the tool must also have a radius. It is also important that one cutting edge should not be in advance of the other.

The parting tool should be held vertically on the oiled sharpening stone and rubbed to and fro to ensure that both cutting edges will be in the same plane (B). The excess oil should then be

figure 13

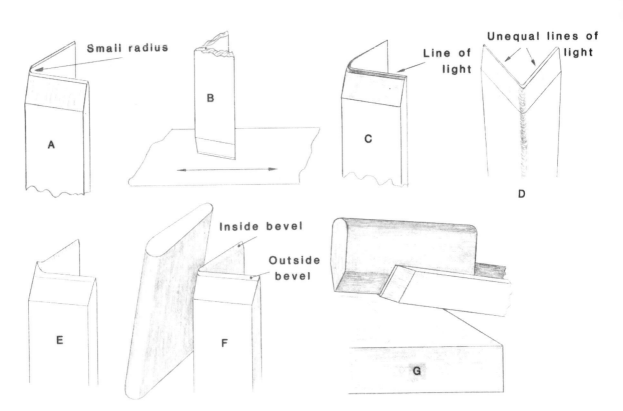

wiped from the tool and the cutting edge will then be shown as a line of light (C). If this line of light is wider in some places than others (D), it indicates that there is uneven sharpening, with excess metal in some places which will have to be worn away on the sharpening stone to obtain two equal bevels.

Honing the outside bevels of this tool requires a similar technique to that of sharpening a chisel, but it will be seen that after honing, a hook is formed (E) which has to be removed. The hook is formed where the inside vee, which has a small radius, meets the outside vee, which has no radius. Removing this hook may be done on the bench stone or with a slipstone (F).

Sharpening the inside bevels of the parting tool requires a slipstone which fits comfortably into the angle of the vee, and the technique is similar to that employed for sharpening the inside of the gouge while ensuring that the tool is supported on the edge of the bench (G). The final sharpening is carried out on the strop by drawing the tool along the edge of the leather.

Principles of sharpening described thus far apply equally to all cutting tools of the edge type, namely drawknife, spokeshave, knives etc.

All craftsmen require sharp tools, but the methods used to obtain the sharp edge vary from craftsman to craftsman. For instance, if it is difficult to maintain the correct angle when passing the tool over the surface of the sharpening stone, as described in sharpening a chisel, then a sideways motion may prove easier. It does not matter too much how the tool is sharpened. It is its cutting capability that counts. Time taken to sharpen tools may be wasted if not enough care is taken to prevent accidental damage. A tool roll (canvas holdall) or felt-lined tool tray is the best place for tools not being used.

Sharpening a Scraper

The method sequence in figure 14 shows a curved-edged scraper held in a vice with a half round fine cut file being used to shape the edge. To minimise the file marks, the edge should be draw-filed, that is the file is drawn along the edge in the same manner as the round slipstone in the next diagram.

The ticketer or burnisher is a bar of hardened steel which is used to form a burr. It is drawn several times along the sides of the scraper to raise the initial burr and for this operation the tool is laid flat on the bench with as much pressure as possible being applied to the steel bar.

figure 14

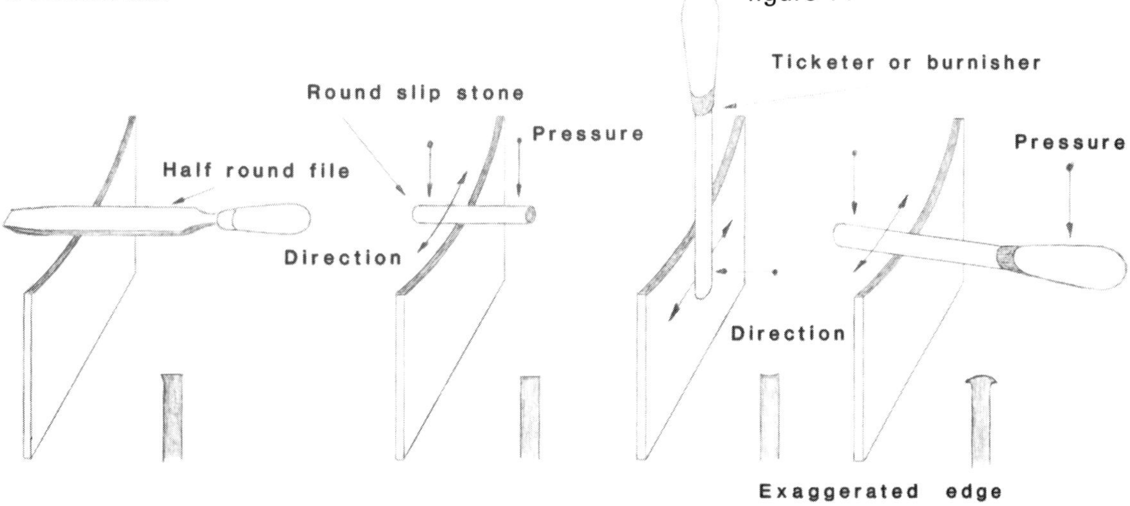

Half round file

Round slip stone

Pressure

Direction

Ticketer or burnisher

Pressure

Direction

Exaggerated edge

Forming the actual cutting edge requires, first of all, the scraper being returned to the vice. The ticketer is then drawn several times along the cutting edge and this, coupled with a gradual lowering of the ticketer's handle, rolls the metal corner over to form a very fine hook on the edge which does the cutting.

Sharpening Saws (figure 15)
Before any attempt is made to sharpen the teeth of a saw, it is necessary to ensure that the edge of the teeth form a straight line. By holding the saw in a vice with two stout pieces of timber acting as stiffeners for the thin steel (A), and traversing a fine flat file, without its handle, along the teeth, a datum is obtained for the shaping of the teeth (B).

The triangular saw file (F) is correctly shaped for the teeth (C) but it has to be held at an angle to the saw. Rip saw teeth are sharpened straight across, so the file is held at 90° to the saw blade (D), but the cross cut, having different shaped teeth, is held at 60° (E). A saw set (H) bends the tips of the teeth to an angle (G) which provides clearance for the saw when it is cutting.

figure 15

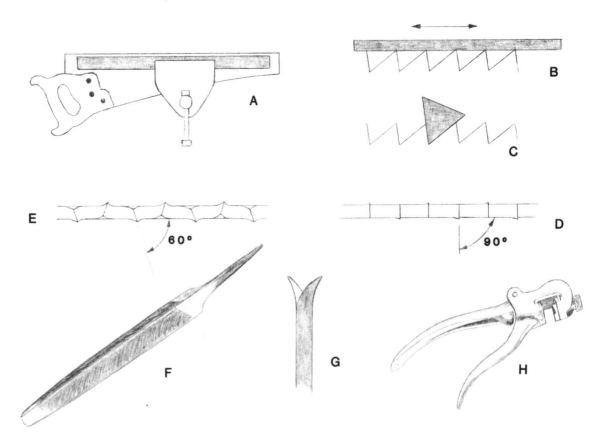

58

7 Experimentation and Improvisation

Improvisation is often useful when an expensive tool is required for only infrequent use. Experimenting with those tools available can widen the potential of the craftsman's equipment without wasting money.

Consider clamping a piece of wood to the bench, say, for a relief carving. A 'G' clamp is probably the easiest tool to use but, if one is not available, another way has to be found and the use of simple clamping blocks (figure 1) may be the answer. These may be made of metal (A) or hardwood (B), and bolts and nuts obtainable from engineers' suppliers or hardware stores will provide the pressure. A simple sash clamp (C) may be made by using folding wooden wedges, but a stout piece of wood is required for the long bar to prevent it bending.

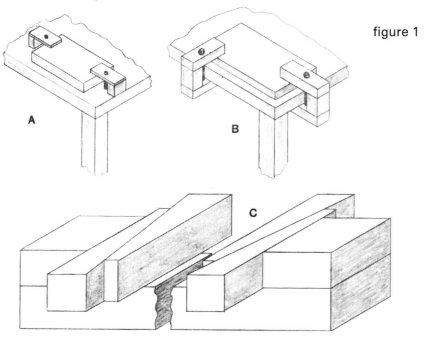

figure 1

A small chisel or gouge can be made from an old screwdriver. The hardness of the tool will probably not be as good as a proprietary make, but it will keep its edge long enough to make the effort worthwhile. The forming of an old screwdriver into a gouge will require heat, and the sequence of operations is shown in figure 2. A steel bar of the required curvature is firmly held in the vice. A blowlamp is applied to the end of the screwdriver until it reaches red heat (A) when it is forged with a hammer (B) over the end of the bar. It may require a number of re-heatings to obtain the shape needed. Oxide, which forms on the surface of the metal, is now cleaned off with an old file or abrasive paper (C) and the tool is reheated until it becomes cherry red in colour (D). As soon as this colour is reached, it is quickly quenched (E) in oil or water. This hardens the tool but makes it very brittle and, to reduce this, the tool has to be tempered. Oxide is again cleaned off (F), more carefully this time, so that the colour changes from heating can be readily observed. The heat source is applied at a little distance from the actual edge (G) so that the straw colour, which appears at the early stage of heating, may be seen to travel towards the cutting edge. Immediately the straw colour reaches the edge, the tool is quenched again (H).

The finishing of awkward places presents a challenge to all sculptors. A piece of abrasive paper glued to a thin piece of wood

figure 2

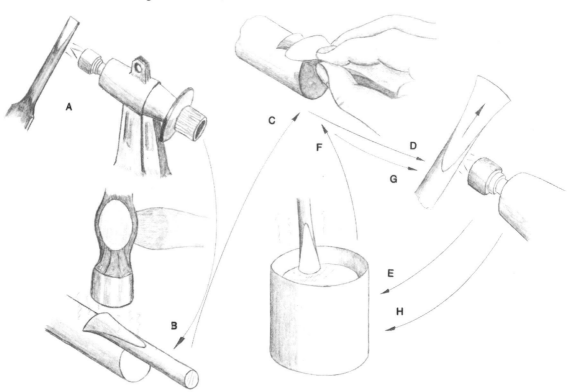

(a lollipop stick) makes a good file and a 60 or 80 grit abrasive paper is almost the equivalent of a riffler. Hacksaw blades may be ground to make very effective small scrapers.

Such things as double-sided adhesive tape have numerous uses: flat pieces of wood may be held in place while they are being worked, and abrasive papers may be attached to sanding blocks.

Woodcarving tools will occasionally get broken, and the broken pieces are excellent material for improvised tools. Woodcarving tools themselves should be studied to determine the shape of cut the tool is capable of. A shallow gouge, for example, normally cuts a curved surface. It will also cut close up to a corner or even a right-angled corner, as the tool profile cuts show in figure 3.

figure 3

8 Abrasive Papers and Adhesives

ABRASIVE PAPER

To the sculptor who demands perfection in wood finish, abrasive products are very important and deserve special consideration. Choosing the right paper for the job can save considerable time and effort. The cutting edge of abrasive paper is provided by very angular and sharp mineral grains which are bonded to the paper backing. The grain sizes are graded and, because of the particular properties of the minerals used, are recommended for differing application.

Silicone Carbide derives from a mixture of quartz and other materials. It is the hardest yet most brittle of the abrasives. It is recommended for medium/soft wood and is available in sheets or rolls with the following grit sizes: 180, 120, 100, 80, 60, 50, 40, 35, 30, 24.

Aluminium Oxide, which is softer but tougher, derives from bauxite and is recommended for rapid stock removal. It is available in sheets or rolls with the following grit sizes: 320, 280, 240, 220, 180, 120, 100, 80, 60, 50, 40, 35, 30, 24.

Garnet, the next hardest, is a single mineral recommended for fine finishing and polishing. It is available in sheets with the following grit sizes, the figure in ( ) indicating the paper designation: 240 (7/0), 220 (6/0), 180 (5/0), 150 (4/0), 120 (3/0), 100 (2/0), 80 (0), 60 (½), 50 (1), 40 (1½).

Glass paper is recommended for cabinet work and general woodworking. It is available in the following grit sizes, the figure in ( ) indicating the paper designation: 240 (FL(Flour)), 220 (0), 150 (1), 120 (1½), 100 (F2), 60 (M2), 40 (S2), 36 (2½), 30 (3).

One other abrasive paper that is very useful to the sculptor is the **resin bonded silicone carbide** paper which is commonly referred to as *wet or dry* and available in grit sizes as fine as 1200. The fine papers are very flexible, giving them a certain advantage when finishing complicated shapes. They are also useful on painted sculpture which has to be rubbed down wet between coats.

The author's own recommendation for the sculptor is to have a stock of 80 and 120 silicone carbide paper for rough sanding softer woods, and a stock of 80 and 120 aluminium oxide paper for harder woods. For finishing work use either garnet or aluminium oxide in grit sizes of 180 and 240 together with *wet or dry* paper in 400 and 600 grit.

Finally, although different papers are recommended for various specific stages in sanding, the sculptor does not have to follow these recommendations to the letter. If the correct papers are not available at the time, any type of coarse, medium and fine abrasive paper will produce the necessary finish, although not necessarily in the most efficient manner.

ADHESIVES

Glue is used as a tool for running repairs and laminating. Although its use is often frowned on by the purist, it is essential if many hours of work are not to be wasted. Glues for uniting or bonding surfaces together are chosen according to prevailing circumstances. Mechanical adhesion, as far as wood is concerned, is the interlocking of the adhesive with the pores or irregularities of the surfaces being joined.

Fish Glue is the adhesive supplied in tubes which is very useful for small work.

Casein, which derives from chemically treated milk curd, is a good strong glue which is supplied as a powder to be mixed with water. Resistant to dry heat and moisture, it has an alkali content which is liable to stain the wood, making it unsuitable for polished sculpture.

Synthetic Resin Adhesives

Adhesives derived from petroleum have advantages over natural products, providing better resistance to moisture and mould growth.

Urea-Formaldehyde is for joints where stress is involved such as bent laminations. It does not stain and, being a powder to mix with water, is quite convenient. Gap filling is another advantage that it possesses.

Phenol-Formaldehyde is an extremely durable glue which is unaffected by weather or even boiling water.

Resorcinal-Formaldehyde is an improvement on the Phenolic, being less sensitive to temperature, and water soluble until cured. This adhesive is recommended for sculpture which is to be painted and situated outdoors or where dampness prevails.

Polyvinyl Acetate is probably the most used of all adhesives. It is ready for use, non-staining, often white in colour, with indefinite storage life and, being water soluble, is very clean to use. This is suitable for sculpture which is not to be exposed to the elements or stress.

Epoxy Resins are very useful for bonding metals and glass, and other mixed media.

Bonding

Cleanliness is an essential part of any gluing operation and an abraded or roughened surface provides a better key for the glue. Care has to be taken not to roughen the surfaces too much otherwise the glue line will become obvious.

Pressure

Pressure is needed to exclude air trapped between the glued surfaces. For small objects, hand pressure might be sufficient but, in most cases, mechanical means are employed, such as a vice, G clamps or sash clamps. A rubbed joint is very efficient if the workpiece is not too large to handle. The joint in figure 1 involved the bringing together of the wet glued surfaces and either rubbing or wringing them together. The sliding of the surfaces expels the air and allows the pressure of the atmosphere to act on the wood.

figure 1

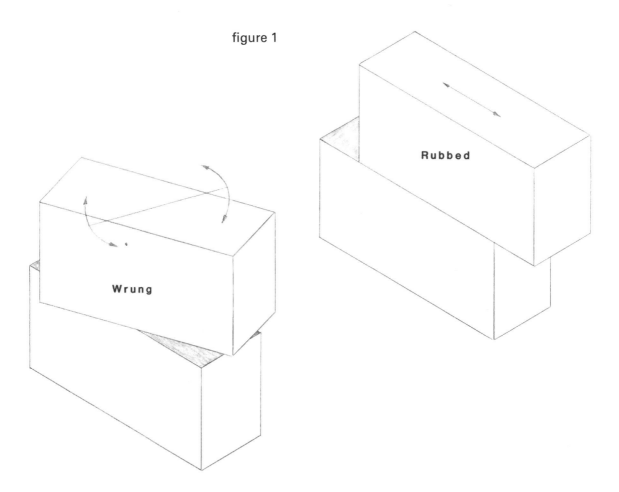

Rubbed

Wrung

III Timber

9 The Raw Material

Timber, the basic material of the wood sculptor, is a very complicated piece of biological engineering, and its structure requires a certain amount of understanding to enable the sculptor to use the material to his advantage. It is not proposed to go into too much detail here except to explain the growth of a tree and its behavioural pattern when felled.

Trying to understand nature is a help towards the understanding and appreciation of any art form. Looking at a section of the tree, the pith may be seen at the centre (figure 1).

figure 1

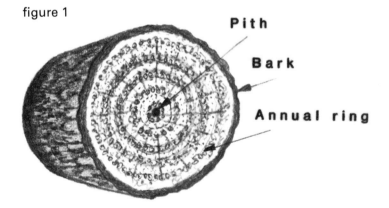

This is where the growth of the tree first started and each year a layer of timber is added to this. The layer of timber comprises two rings of different densities, one of which was formed in the spring and the other in the summer, the summer growth being slower and consequently more compact. It is this summer growth which is referred to as the annual ring. The tree has an overcoat of bark which serves as a protection for a layer of cellular tissue known as the cambium. Cells inside this layer convey the sap up the tree, whereas the cells on the outside, which form the inner layer of bark (known as *bast*), convey food from the leaves down the trunk to the roots.

If the structure of the timber is regarded as a compact bundle of straws (cells) – short for hardwoods and long for softwoods – with periodic lateral ones (rays), an idea is presented to show how this cellular structure not only gives the wood its strength but also provides the grain pattern. The cells do not grow vertically in a straight line and, although the rays generate from the centre of the tree, they too are not straight. Hence when a longitudinal cut is made along a log of wood, the cross section reveals the *grain pattern* (figure 2) and *figure*, if the cut is made at or near the centre where the rays generating from the centre of the tree have been cut through (figure 3).

figure 2

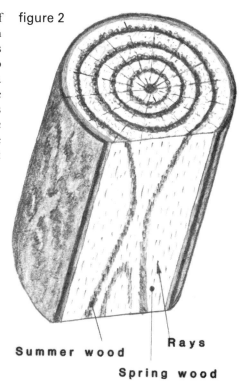

figure 3

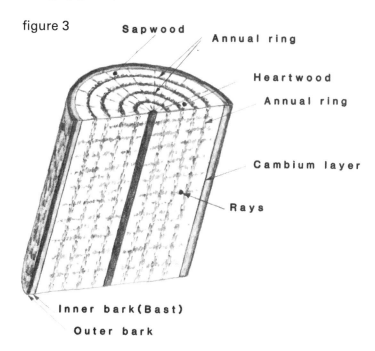

Sapwood

Annual ring

Heartwood

Annual ring

Cambium layer

Rays

Inner bark (Bast)

Outer bark

Summer wood

Rays

Spring wood

Section through centre of tree

Hardwood and softwood are two misnomers, since there are soft hardwoods and hard softwoods. Hardwoods are broad leaved trees such as oak, elm, ash etc.; softwoods are needle leaved trees such as pines (also referred to as conifers). The cellular structure of hardwood is more complex than that of softwood, as can be seen in the highly magnified diagram (figure 4). The cells in softwood are arranged symmetrically in radial rows, whereas hardwood is of fibrous construction with large cells or vessels together with small ones. The diagram has the longitudinal sections on the left and the cross sections on the right.

This brief description of the structure of timber gives little

67

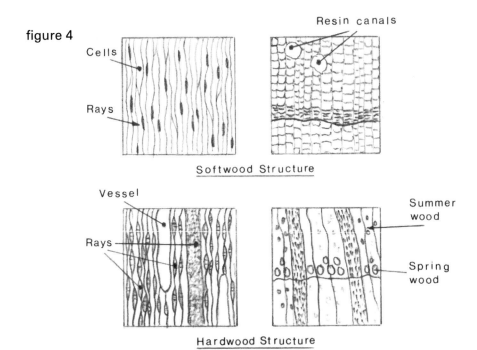

figure 4

Cells

Rays

Resin canals

Softwood Structure

Vessel

Rays

Summer wood

Spring wood

Hardwood Structure

enough information for the technologist, but it will help to explain why timber behaves as it does when it is felled and converted for use by the craftsman. Using timber for sculpture can be an adventure. The sculptor has an idea of what he wants to carve or construct, but there is always the question of whether the timber will let him do just what he wants. Timber is only predictable up to a point: there is a behaviour pattern which it follows but which offers no guarantee.

Before leaving the subject of the structure of timber, there is one practical aspect which should be considered. That is the way in which the timber behaves with the application of the different cutting tools. Comparison was made earlier between the structure of wood and a bundle of straws. Imagine that each straw is bonded to the next and represents the fibrous or cellular construction of wood. If a cut is made with a chisel, in an attempt to follow the dotted line (figure 5), the tool will cut well on the downward direction but, when changing direction, the cutting edge acts as a wedge, the fibres separate and the assembly splits. Conclusion: the tool will cut easily in the direction of grain.

Imagine cutting across the same bundle of straws. This time a gouge is the tool and the cut is made toward the centre from each side (figure 6). Observation shows that if the tool was allowed to continue right across the bundle, the straws at the end of the cut tended to split (figure 7), but if approached from each side there was no problem. Conclusion: the tool will cut easily across the grain but care has to be taken when reaching the end of the cut.

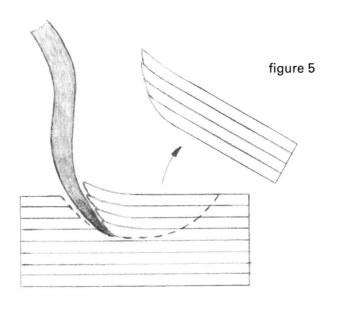

figure 5

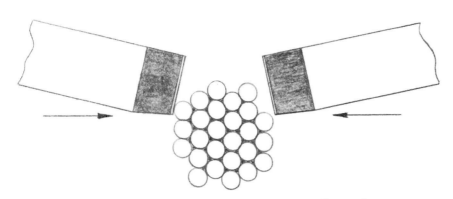

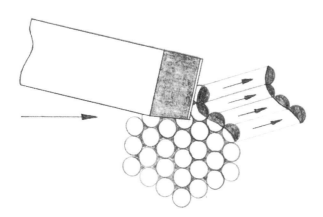

figure 6

figure 7

10 Seasoning

Seasoning is drying out the moisture contained in the wood to a level conducive to its proposed use. This should be carried out initially either very slowly in the open air, or under the controlled conditions of a kiln, and the degree of seasoning is measured by the moisture content of the wood as a percentage of the dry weight of the timber.

Shrinkage occurs in the cell walls as the moisture content reduces. The sapwood, which contains far more moisture than the heartwood, consequently loses moisture more rapidly and this sets up uneven shrinkage, causing splits and shakes to develop.

figure 1

Timber cut as this diagram illustrates (figure 1) will experience

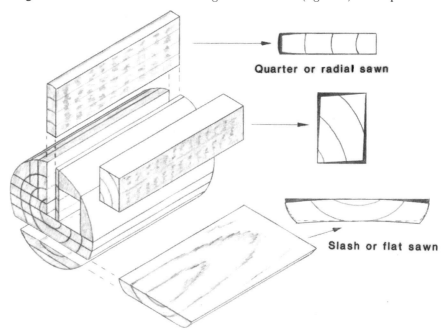

Quarter or radial sawn

Slash or flat sawn

Shrinkage and movement expected from drying

the shrinkage and movement shown. Quarter sawn timber has been cut radially, or as near to this as the sawyer can practicably get, to produce timber with similar length growth rings. This results in a more stable piece of wood. Compare this with the wood that is slash sawn and it will be seen that, as shrinkage takes place along the annual rings, these rings shorten and force the wood to take up the shape shown. This is also the case in the section from the top quarter.

The sculptor usually requires a large piece of timber for even quite small work and he will not be in a position to select his timber in the same way as the cabinet-maker. However, he will be able to study the growth rings and forecast how the timber will behave before deciding if a particular piece of material is suitable for the work he has in mind. The sculptor should try to avoid timber which includes the pith because it is around this point that distortion takes place. In figure 2 it will be seen that the stress set up by shrinkage has caused the log to split whereas the log which was quartered is free to move and much less likely to split.

figure 2

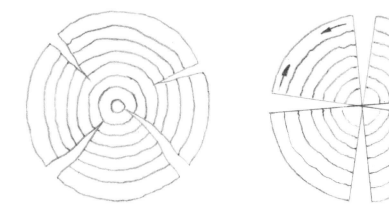

The effects of uneven shrinkage compared with a log which has been quartered

KILN SEASONING

Kiln seasoning is a rapid method where water-saturated air is circulated in a heated chamber. Over a period of time, the heat is increased and the humidity decreased. Kiln seasoned timber used for sculpture should be sealed to prevent moisture absorption. Timber is hygroscopic and its moisture content will adjust to ambient conditions. If the wood is sealed and left in the studio for a few weeks before starting to cut into it, less trouble might be expected. It is a wise precaution to seal finished work before leaving it in a centrally heated environment for any length of time (see Chapter 20 on finishing techniques). Remember always that the moisture content of wood is continually changing, according to the temperature and humidity of the environment, and so the controlled atmosphere of modern buildings is most amenable since the timber is less liable to split.

AIR SEASONING

Seasoning in air is a very slow process and a rule of thumb is 9 – 12 months per 25mm (1in.) of thickness. Ventilation is essential as is shelter from both rain and sun. The planks of timber are stacked off the ground with sticks about 0.5m (20in.) apart separating each plank. To prevent the ends splitting, they are coated with paint or paraffin wax which prevents too rapid evaporation from the end grain (figure 3). Logs are dealt with similarly by sealing the ends and separating each log from the next. The moisture content for air seasoned timber may start in excess of 27% and reduce to 17% (approximately).

figure 3

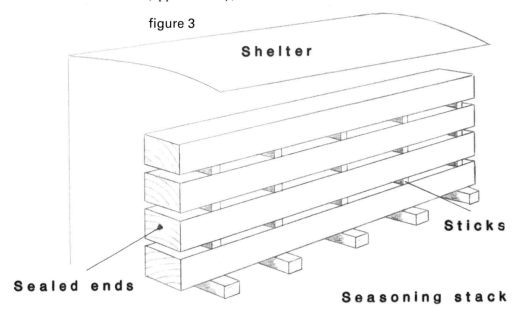

Shelter

Sticks

Sealed ends

Seasoning stack

The moisture content of acclimatised timber in a centrally heated house is approximately 11% but, depending on location, may be as low as 8%, so it will be seen that problems can develop if care is not taken when the wood is brought into the house. Precautions to combat the effects of this change in environment will vary. Humidity plays an important part, so it is important not to expose the timber to a drier atmosphere too soon or for too long. A cool ventilated part of the house should be chosen to finish off the seasoning, especially if the timber is to be worked on in the house. The wood should be returned to the same place after each work

1 'Otter' by Ron Lane. This was carved from one piece; the wood
is imbuya walnut from Brazil. When first cut, the wood has a
rich orange colour, but this soon darkens when exposed to the light.
250mm (10 in.)

3 'Cormorant' by Ron Lane was carved from a piece of English walnut. 500mm (20 in.)

2 'Rosebud' by Ron Lane. The bud was carved from American redwood, the sepals and stem from acacia, and it is set in walnut. 200mm (8 in.)

period. A garden studio which is heated only for the working period presents fewer problems, but a warning must be given about placing the wood too close to the heating source.

A visit to galleries and museums is an education into the behaviour of timber. It will be seen that wood carvings which contain the heart or pith of the tree will probably have developed shakes or splits generating from the centre. Very old church carvings will have hollow backs which help avoid this problem.

It should be said here that these defects which detract from the appearance of the finished work, should not deter the sculptor from executing the ideas that he wishes to put into practice. Certain defects in sculpture are acceptable, especially in large works. If the sculptor needs to use a certain piece of timber to produce a certain form, nature's reaction is often unavoidable. This photograph of a work by Barbara Hepworth (figure 4) is a good illustration of both faulty seasoning and wrong choice of timber. The timber used was a very large section of holly. The effects of the bad seasoning are obvious, but a later edition of the same form executed in plane had no such disastrous results. This statement is not meant in any way to denigrate the work of Barbara Hepworth. Rather, it is a fine example of where even the best of craftsmen will admit to making a mistake.

figure 4

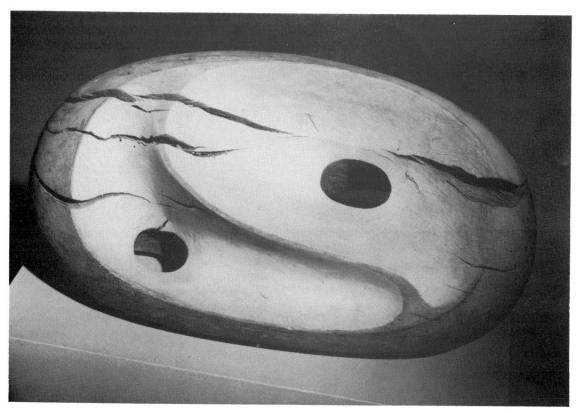

figure 5

A practical example of the effects of drying out or seasoning is shown in the following description of a yew bowl (figure 5), made by a wood sculpture student. The sculptor wanted to produce a salad bowl, and the outside of the log was so attractive and intriguing that he decided to retain this natural form as a feature of the finished work.

The yew log had been air dried for three years and, if kept in an unchanging humidity, might have withstood the rigours of being hollowed out without developing shakes or splits. (Since this was a student project, which was worked on for only a short period each week, there was a large element of risk involved.) It was decided at the start that the work would be stored in the same environment as when drying out and only brought indoors for the few hours' work period each week. The hollowing out of the bowl did not become a problem until approaching the full depth, when circumstances had to be considered again. Working with the mallet also induced stress that made it necessary to take lighter cuts. The ever-increasing surface area of the carved section meant that considerable movement could be expected in this region whilst, at the same time, imposing stresses on the base of the bowl that could only be relieved by the shakes that would develop. There was a choice to be made: either the wood that had been carved could be sealed each time (see Chapter 20) to prevent further loss of moisture during the week, or a risk could be taken and the student could carry on, hoping that the wood would not split. It was an equitable time of the year so it was decided to carry on.

It was not until the finished depth was almost reached that there was any sign of splitting and, when this did occur, it was not surprising or discouraging. It was realised from the beginning that this might happen and the student was prepared for his finished work to become a bowl for holding fresh fruit, instead of a salad bowl where moisture could penetrate the crack, and it must be agreed that it does not detract from the appearance of the finished work (figure 6).

Once again, the natural form of the outside of the bowl is aesthetically compatible with the shake which appeared naturally.

figure 6

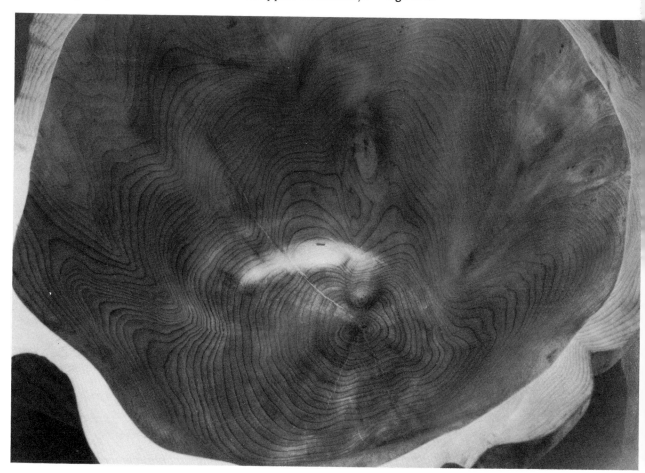

11 Suitable Types of Wood for Carving

It is true to say that most timbers can be carved, but some do require a high degree of skill to shape. The timbers available that are easy to carve, such as lime and pear, are perhaps best suited for the more intricate carvings, whereas others with wild or pronounced grain patterns may inspire other types of sculpture, perhaps more abstract in form. If possible, it is as well to try any timber that comes to hand and attempt to overcome any obstacles which present themselves.

Pear and lime respond beautifully to sharp tools, and give encouraging results which are particularly gratifying to the beginner. This is not to say, however, that the novice should be discouraged from using other timbers, but it must be borne in mind that different timbers have different characteristics, and it may require some practice or previous knowledge to know which wood is most suitable for the proposed work.

TIMBER SUPPLY

There are various sources of supply for suitable carving timbers and once the carver gets established and his work known, he will probably be offered more than he can use. The beginner, however, will probably find it easier to contact a local timber merchant or importer for his initial supply. These suppliers are usually sympathetic to students of wood carving and have small supplies of suitable timber.

There is a number of firms advertising suitable timbers in the woodworking magazines, and practitioners of the craft are well advised to subscribe to these magazines to help keep abreast of their subject. Tree surgeons, landscape gardeners, estate workers, forestry workers – these are the people who can often help with supplies of home-grown timbers, as are the home-grown timber merchants situated in many of our rural areas.

Local woods or forests often reveal the more unusual shaped branches or roots, but the rule is never to cut growing timber. The wind and other natural causes will provide wood that has been drying naturally in the air and lying on the forest floor, waiting for someone to reveal the beauty underneath the bark.

LAMINATED TIMBER

Laminated timber is panels or blocks of wood that have been glued, pinned or dowelled together. The reasons for building up timber in this way may be for strength and economy, as is the case with plywood or blockboard, or for making up large blocks of wood suitable for large sculpture. This method may also be used to build up sections to ensure that the grain directions are running the correct way, for work such as the tern in figure 1. In this example,

figure 1

the grain direction of one piece of wood follows the beak of the bird, a second follows the tail, whereas the grain in the wings is at right-angles to the body. Texturing the surface of the wood by burning with a pyrography tool has made the joints less obvious. This is a case where the work has been carved from blocks of wood which have been joined together, with the grain direction of each piece running the best way to give strength to the work.

When gluing together wood that has the grain direction running the same way, the annual ring pattern at the end of the wood should be studied. As shrinkage takes place, there is a tendency for the rings to try and straighten but, if the wood is arranged as this diagram (figure 2) shows, the shrinkage forces are opposed to one another and so there is little or no change in the overall shape.

figure 2

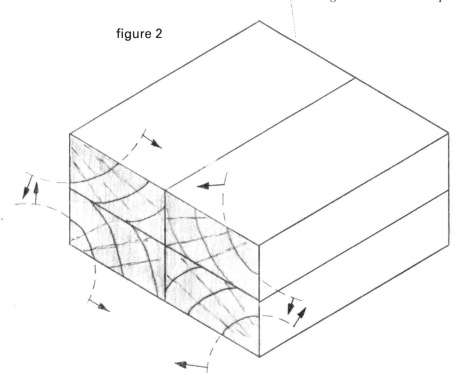

Arrows indicating shrinkage forces

Figure 3 shows two pieces of wood which have been bonded together with their respective grain directions running at right-angles to each other. The expected shrinkage at A will be greater than that at B and, because of this, the glued joint must be strong enough to resist this movement. In this situation it is worth considering giving the glue some assistance. Wooden dowels, shown as dotted lines in the diagram, would help to absorb some

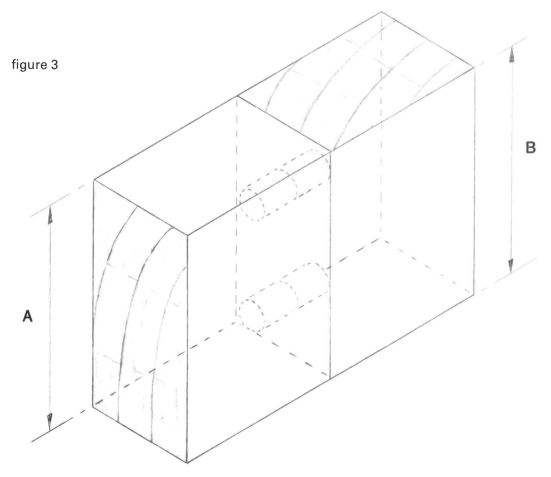

figure 3

of the shrinkage force, but the best help will come from siting the finished work in an environment which is not subject to dramatic humidity changes.

Laminated timber extends the horizons of the sculptor, especially if his work is to be painted or the joints disguised in some way. Figureheads on ships were carved for many years using this method, the wood being dry-jointed and dowelled together.

MIXED MEDIA

Mixed media is a term applied to sculpture made up of an assortment of materials. This is frowned on by the purist, but there is often no alternative if the message conveyed by the work is to be understood.

Barbara Hepworth's sculpture 'Pelagos' (figure 4) shows how polished wood, paint and strings can present a harmonious study of form. The surface shape, with strings suggesting the geometric development, together with the contrasting colour of the paint,

80

figure 4

direct the eye of the viewer to a concordant whole that is acceptable and full of interest.

The author's carved birds are a more modest illustration of mixed media where the use of steel, synthetics and scorched wood combine to create an impression of a bird form that is acceptable to the eye for the realism that is conveyed.

There are, however, instances where the mixing of media would be out of place, and this beautiful study of a bird by Derek George (figure 5) is one such case. Derek is well known for his exploitation of the grain pattern of the wood for conveying the features of his birds. He goes to great lengths to find timber which has a grain pattern that is compatible with the natural characteristics of the bird. It is because of this, together with the natural appearance of the timber, that any other media, used in conjunction with the composition, would detract from the whole. The eye accepts what is natural which, in this instance, is natural form and natural wood.

The use of mixed media often provides a means of expression and helps towards the appeal of the finished article. The type of finish, choice of tool and shape of the work all play an important part, and there are no rules to prevent their exploitation. The

figure 5

sculptor need never fear the use of mixed media or lamination in his work, if he thinks of Gianlorenzo Bernini (1598-1680), who used combinations of laminated marble, bronze and polychrome, together with light and shade produced by strategically placed windows. His baldacchino in St Peter's Basilica, Rome, shows all of these to glorious effect.

The following table has been compiled to provide information on those timbers with which the sculptor may become involved. Recommendations for the type of work for which each particular timber is suited have been based on the workability of the wood, together with its appearance or grain pattern. 'Abstract', as far as this table is concerned, is the production of sculptural form devoid of fine detail.

Timber	Colour	Remarks	Recommendations	Density	
				Kg/m^3	lb/ft^3
Agba	Pink to brown	Coarse grain	Abstracts	512	32
Apple	White	Close grain	Small carvings	770	48
Ash	White to pale brown	Coarse grain	Abstracts	738	46
Beech	Pale brown	Close grain	Detailed carvings	707	44
Box	Pale cream	Dense, close grain	Small detailed carvings	1044	65
Cherry	Pale pink to brown	Close grain	Small carvings	626	39
Chestnut (Sweet)	Pale brown	Coarse grain	Detailed carvings	450	28
Douglas Fir	Cream to brown	Dense growth rings	Abstracts	530	33
Ebony	Brown to black	Dense, close grain, very hard	Detailed carvings	1221	76
Elm	Light brown	Coarse grain	Abstracts	578	36
Holly	White	Close grain	Small detailed carvings	755	47
Iroko	Brown	Close, interlocked grain	Abstracts or detailed carvings	675	42
Jelutong	Cream	Close but uninteresting grain pattern	Carvings that are painted or textured	481	30
Laburnum	Cream to dark brown	Dense, close grain	Abstracts or detailed carvings	803	50
Lime	Pale cream	Close grain	Detailed carvings	594	37
Mahogany	Reddish brown	Fairly close to close grain	Abstracts or detailed carvings	481-642 (depending on species)	30-40
Oak	Pale brown	Coarse grain	Detailed carvings	787	49
Obeche	Cream	Fairly close grain	Small carvings	385	24
Padauk	Red	Open grain, often interlocked	Abstracts	867	54
Parana Pine	Cream to red	Uninteresting grain pattern	Abstracts	544	34
Pear	Pale brown	Close grain	Detailed carvings	755	47
Purpleheart	Dark brown to purple	Close grain	Abstracts or detailed carvings	913	57
Redwood or Scots Pine	Pale yellow to brown	Requires sharp tools	Abstracts	418	26
Rosewood	Brown to almost black	Close grain	Abstracts	883	55
Sycamore	White	Close grain	Abstracts or detailed carvings	610	38
Teak	Brown	Open grain, oily	Abstracts	723	45
Walnut	Brown	Fairly close grain	Abstracts or detailed carvings	691	43
Yellow Pine	Pale yellow	Close grain	Abstracts or detailed carvings	418	26
Yew	White to red	Interlocked grain	Abstracts or detailed carvings	787	49

IV Design and Technique

12 Design

Successful design concludes with the manufacture of something that is at once pleasing to the eye and the hand, whilst also carrying out its function effectively. The main criterion in sculpture is appearance and this involves a study of the material used in addition to the subject itself. If a sculptural work becomes a conversation piece, in the sense that the observers have a genuine interest in the work itself and the sculptor in particular, then it may be said that the work is successful.

FUNCTION IN DESIGNING

Certain problems face furniture designers, since their work is primarily functional, with aesthetics coming a close second. They have to study the timber used in construction, the methods of construction and their influence on the appearance of the finished product. The piece of furniture must be strong enough to withstand the demands put upon it and, at the same time, have a visual appeal that satisfies the purchasers of the piece.

The function, therefore, is a consideration in any design, and each piece of work will have a purpose. Sometimes the purpose may be as obscure as the appearance of the work of art itself, promoting discussion and conjecture.

COMMUNICATION

There is a strong desire to communicate with a piece of sculpture. The shape and finish draw the hand of the observer, if he is close enough to touch it, whilst the eyes absorb the detail, if the work is far away. It is for this reason that the form or shape should have an interesting *feel*. Sculptures should be tactile, as in an animal carving where the shoulders, thighs and backbone have a definitive shape discernable by touch. The purchase of one of the author's carved birds by a totally blind person demonstrates this quality.

The sculptor uses every aspect of his work for communication. The finish of the work may have something to say, for instance. If a sculpture is left with a tool finish only, the observer may at first glance think that the work is unfinished but, with a little thought, he will realise that the artist has taken his finish far enough to convey his message and any more effort would serve no purpose.

'The Cormorants' by William Graveney (figure 1) is undoubtedly an example of natural expression. The tooled finish creates an impression of the birds having just left the water. Their bedraggled appearance lends emphasis to the very lifelike form of the carving. Although the observer may think that the work is unfinished because the tool cuts are roughly done, the sculptor has deliberately not taken the finish any further because, by sanding and polishing the wood, he would have created conflict between the beauty of the grain pattern and the form of the carving.

figure 1

Much may be learned from past masters of sculpture. Look at Michelangelo's works and the way he left a rough hole for a curl of hair or the pupil of an eye. The holes were left unashamedly: there was no need for the hole to be polished to the same extent as the rest of the sculpture. On the other hand, the 'Pietà' in St Peter's Basilica, Rome, combines the classical beauty of form with the natural beauty of the marble in such a way that the drilling of the sculpture required polishing to tone in with the rest of the work. This is perhaps the exception to Michelangelo's usual portrayal, where body form was generally emphasised by exaggeration.

Moving on now to present-day initiates of the craft, the question of design promotes the same problems. The craftsman is required to portray the subject-matter in a way that appeals not only to himself, but also to the people who will be looking at his work. The sculpture, in a manner of speaking, has to say something. It may be a simple message, where the sculpture is a copy of the real thing, as in a scale model recording the detail of the original subject, or the same subject may be portrayed not only in detail, but in a position which suggests function, attitude or actions, all of which add even more interest. The same subject might be portrayed in a totally different manner, in a shape or form which is completely meaningless to all but the craftsman. He will have developed the form in a way which appeals to his instincts and, with luck, to the people who look at his work. The message in this instance might be summed up by the word *appeal*, but if the message needs to be examined in depth, then the thoughts and methods of the sculptor will require exposure.

Figure 2 is of 'The Dancer' by Henri Gaudier-Brzeska, and the viewer might be forgiven for thinking of it as being just a dancer, in view of the title. Actually, the sculpture is the result of many hours spent studying the movement and form of the ballet itself and, to appreciate the work more fully, some knowledge of the sculptor is required as well as a detailed study of the form.

Another sculpture by Gaudier-Brzeska is of wrestlers, and this was also the result of a prolonged study of wrestling bouts. A quick sketch artist, he was able to produce a vast number of impressions on paper whilst watching a match and the final sculpture was the result of much thought and effort. A photographic recording might be thought to be a better representation of a ballet or wrestling bout, but the recording is of only one moment in time. Brzeska's work is representative of many performances and covers the whole, both physically and mentally.

A practical example will illustrate the above points on design: a sculpture of the madonna is planned, and the choice of material is between a piece of teak with a strong grain pattern, and lime, which has no pronounced grain pattern. If teak were chosen, an abstract form with emphasis on strong lines and curves would be most suited, since the strong natural grain pattern which displays the tree's growth to best advantage, is something that should not

figure 2

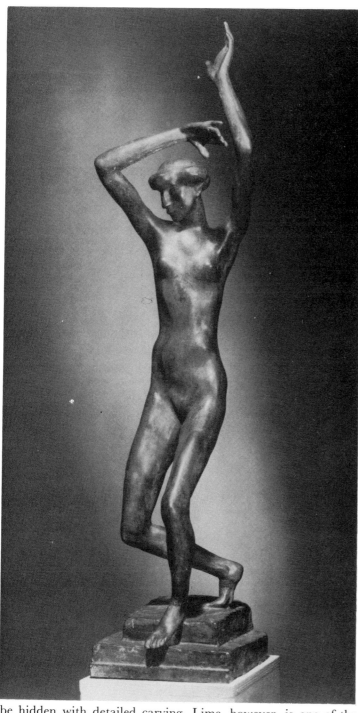

be hidden with detailed carving. Lime, however, is one of the favoured timbers for detail work, and so a finer and more intricate sculpture should result from its natural qualities.

13 Geometry in Sculpture

Geometry has always played a part in constructions of any sort and, more often than not, it is used without realising the function it plays. Architects and engineers use geometric form to give strength to their structures and aesthetic appeal to their designs. An example of this is the vaulted and domed roofs of our churches and cathedrals (figure 1).

To the sculptor, solid and plane geometry offer an infinite number of challenges in form and material. Unlike the architect, he does not have to design a structure which complies with certain criteria; the sculptor makes his own rules regarding shape, methods and materials. Visits to galleries and museums will show

figure 1

that a number of contemporary artists are using geometric form in both painting and sculpture.

Figure 2 shows but a few examples, to give the sculptor food for thought. What has been given here are basic shapes, and the way to exploit them is the prerogative of the sculptor. He may decide to use wire, string or thin wooden laminates to show the development, or he may prefer to carve from solid. The designs have been based on a tetrahedron or triangular pyramid (A), eccentric circles (B), a rectangular prism which has been twisted through 90° (C), the Egyptian cubic form (D) and a hyperbolic paraboloid (E).

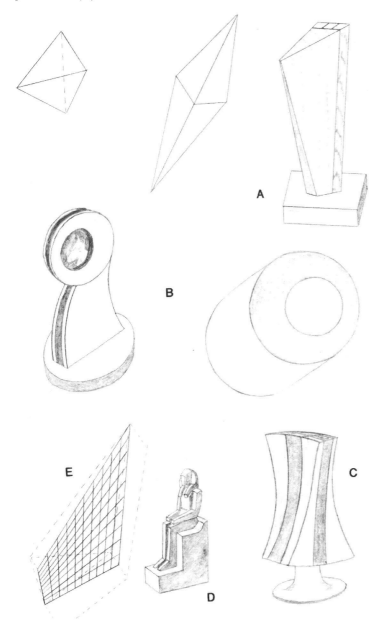

figure 2

14 The Choice of Subject

figure 1

The choice of subject is not usually a problem to the experienced sculptor but the novice may find that a lack of skills, as well as lack of experience, produce limiting factors. Sculptural form is the result of inspiration and this may come from almost any basic idea. Perhaps the craftsman has a fascination for clouds, water, light and shade, the folds of a curtain, hills, sea or anything else inanimate that contains a suggestion of movement (figure 1 by Ron Lane). Still life, animal or insect life may be the source of inspiration.

Portrayal of inanimate subjects means that impressions are created to demonstrate those aspects that the sculptor wants to emphasise. Clouds, for instance, may quite simply be a piece of wood which has been shaped into a copy of a bundle of cotton wool. Water may be thought of as coming from a fountain, where the parabola described by the water spouting will give rise to the creation of an abstract geometric form (figure 2). Light and shade are well illustrated in the vertical columns of Justin Knowles' sculpture 'Steel Forms' (figure 3), where the view constantly changes as the viewer walks around the work. The time of day also plays an important role in light and shade.

figure 2

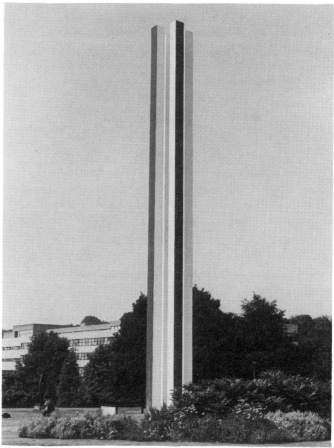

figure 3

An appreciation of nature is the basic requirement of all sculpture. Abstract portrayal of the subject may not appeal to everyone but often it is the only way, especially with the more obscure. Nature's phenomena impose limitations on both materials and craftsmen and, because of this, a certain amount of licence must be granted.

The author's goose (figure 4) is an example of licence where no attempt has been made to produce an exact copy of the bird. The head is not the correct shape and the body is not proportionate, yet the overall effect is that of a goose and the position of the head provides the necessary suggestions of movement. The limitations of nature in this case are the grain of the wood used, which allows only a slight inclination of the head, and the need to exaggerate the thickness of the body to emphasise the body weight. Had this sculpture been produced as a scale model of a goose, using the finishing techniques of the author, it would not look at all realistic. Conversely, had the bird been painted in its natural colours, the emphasis would have been placed on its disproportions, which suggests that in scale model making, it is necessary to copy nature as closely as possible.

figure 4

figure 5

Sculpture does not necessarily have to be only decorative. Furniture and other household items also come within the framework of sculpture, with the functional aspect complementing the design or vice versa, and an example of this may be seen in the carved furniture of Thomas Chippendale (figure 5).

The few examples discussed should enable the beginner to find a subject without too much difficulty. If sculpture is taken seriously then the craftsman will seek his own style of portrayal and probably his own methods for choosing a subject. There is tremendous pleasure to be obtained from researching a subject and deciding how it is to be portrayed, apart from the satisfaction of carving and presentation.

15 Drawing, Scaling and Defining

This chapter deals with people's attitudes toward what they feel is their inability to put a particular shape on to paper, and their difficulties in defining a three-dimensional form.

DRAWING

A fundamental difficulty with drawing is the reason given by many would-be carvers for not attempting a sculpture. There is no denying that the ability to sketch is a decided advantage, but it is not something that need be a real deterrent. There are ways round the problem.

Sculpture is, in effect, drawing in three dimensions. The breadth and depth of the subject can often be obtained from a photograph or painting, if the picture is in profile. The unknown quantity is the width of the subject and it is this dimension that requires some thought and often research. The two examples dealt with in this chapter offer suggestions as to how the problem may be approached, but it must be realised that the results are an approximation of picture content and not an idea for sculpture which has originality.

figure 1

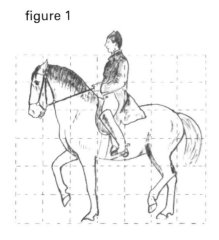

SCALING

Scaling is the reduction or enlarging of an existing drawing or picture, and the method described here is straightforward and effective. Figure 1 is a tracing taken from a postcard of a horse and rider from the Spanish Riding School in Vienna, and what appeals to the sculptor, and what he would like to capture in his finished work, is the pent up energy of the horse without its rider.

The horse and rider, viewed from the side, give the proportions of the horse in this direction, but what it does not show is the detail of the horse viewed from the front. To help determine this detail, another postcard picture provided a front profile which was unfortunately of a different size (figure 2). What the sculptor requires is a profile of the horse when viewed from the side, front and top to the same scale.

For practical purposes, the size of the carving has now to be decided and this of course depends on the wood that is available. Say the depth of the carving is to be 150mm (6in.). It now requires a piece of tracing paper to be marked off into 25mm (1in.) squares, giving six squares depth and a few extra for the breadth. The tracings of the two horses are now divided into a like number of squares. It is sometimes an advantage to number corresponding squares, especially if it is a large or intricate profile that is being prepared. The numbers help in locating positions.

The content of each square is now transferred to the larger tracing paper (figure 3). Using this method, it is not difficult to produce a reasonably accurate drawing of the subject, although an important thing to remember when taking a direct impression of a picture, is that perspective has to be allowed for. The hind legs of the horse, being further away from the camera, appear much smaller than they really are and when the drawings are used for the outlines of the carving, the hind legs must be thickened and lengthened to match the forelegs.

figure 2

figure 3

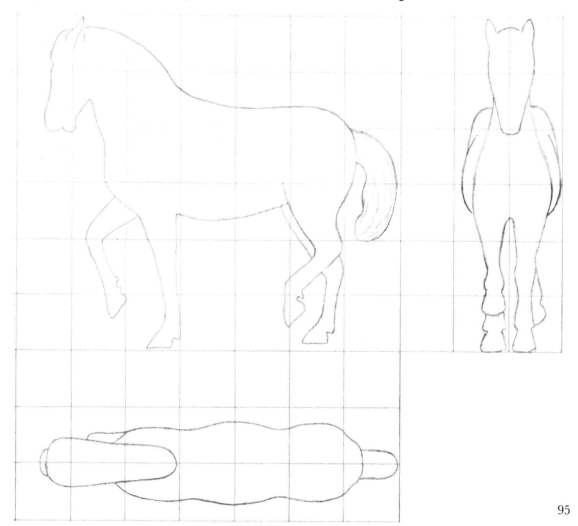

95

So far, what has been obtained is an elevation of the horse together with a view from the front and an assumed view of the rear. The third dimension, a plan or view from above the horse, might be considered necessary, but it requires research to determine the profile. If the views obtained so far are projected as the diagram shows, it is possible to combine information from them to help produce a plan view. Prominent features such as the nose, forehead, belly, thighs and shoulders may be located on the side view and projected down to the plan, whilst the relative position of these on the front view may be estimated by the squares.

The horse is taken a stage further in Chapter 16 where it is used as an example of carving in the round.

DEFINING THE SHAPE OF THE SUBJECT

Mention has been made in the last section of the difficulties encountered in determining the third dimension from a picture. Birds and animals are obviously not all of the same size or shape, but they are nevertheless proportionate, and it is these proportions that have to be ascertained.

Doubts that exist about the shape of the work can be dispelled by obtaining as much information as possible about the shape of the subject, and by making a model with modelling clay which, unlike wood, has the advantage of easy replacement should too much of it be carved away. This modelling material, which could be plasticine, will require a skeleton frame, especially for birds with outstretched wings, to prevent the clay from sagging under its own weight.

Discussion of a practical example illustrates another method of obtaining sufficient information from a picture to construct a model. The duck shown rising from the water in figure 4 is a drawing of a picture in a magazine which, for sculpting purposes, has a number of unknown quantities. The angle of the body and the wings, as presented by the picture, means that the true shapes of both have to be determined before the picture profiles can be transferred to the wood to be carved.

To the artist, the drawing of the elevations will present no problems, but to others a different approach is necessary. In the picture, the angle of inclination of the duck to the horizontal is about 25° and the angle at which it appears to be coming out of the plane of the page is judged to be 30°. If the 25° angle is drawn along the picture of the duck, or a tracing of it, certain strategic parts can be marked on this line. The extremes of the beak, edges of wings, centres of curves etc. are marked, and these same distances transferred to their respective points along the line OJ in figure 5.

Because the picture has only two dimensions, it will be seen that the length of the duck equals the distance AJ in the diagram, but as this length is inclined 30° to the vertical, the true length is A/1 to J/1. Points A to J are now projected at 90° to the line OJ and the

4 'Mare and Foal' by Ron Lane was carved from a well-seasoned yew tree felled in 1914, and set on a slab of rough sap walnut. 200mm (8 in.)

5 'Tern' by Ron Lane was carved from sycamore, with the cap of the head in ebony, and the beak and feet in yew. 300mm (12 in.)

6 'Grey Wagtail' by David Orchard was carved from
jelutong and mounted on serpentine. 150mm (6 in.)

7 'Tern' by David Orchard was carved from jelutong and
mounted on serpentine. 175mm (7 in.)

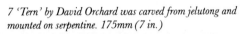

figure 4

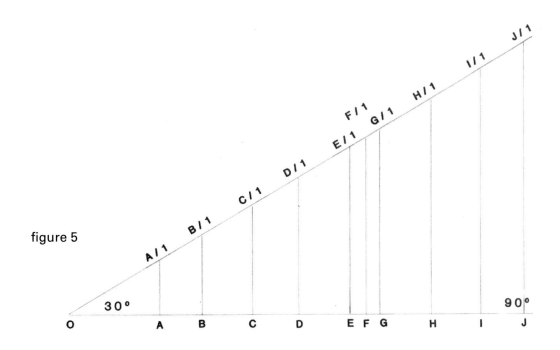

figure 5

97

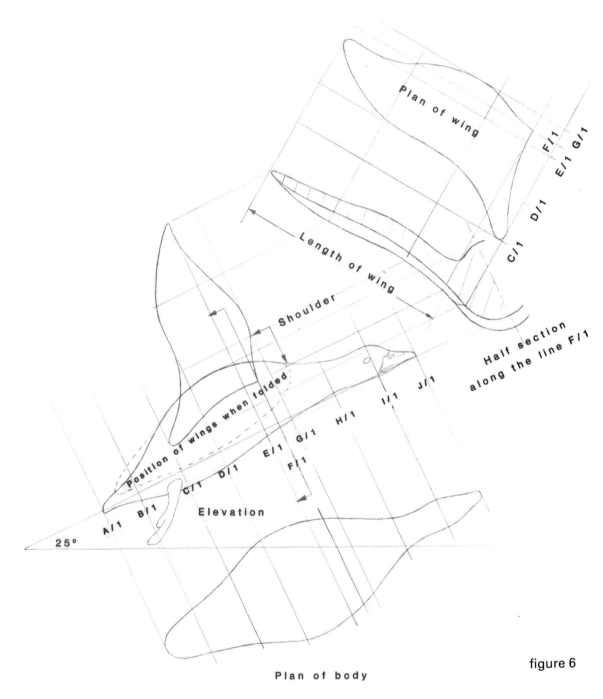

Plan of wing

F/1

C/1 D/1 E/1 G/1

Length of wing

Shoulder

Half section
along the line F/1

Position of wings when folded

E/1 G/1 H/1 I/1 J/1

C/1 D/1

F/1

A/1 B/1 Elevation

25°

Plan of body

figure 6

lengths thus obtained are indicated on the side elevation in figure 6. At each of these points, the picture has to be studied to determine the depth of the line. For instance, A to B in the picture is being viewed from below and because of perspective it implies an untrue depth. The eye-level of the picture is below the subject, so to obtain a more accurate profile of the bird, the draughtsman has to imagine the body being tilted. Research will have shown that the tail in flight is slightly curved in plan but tapered in elevation. The bird's body is oval in section so progression to other points along this line means that approximate body dimensions can be taken directly from the picture. With this information the elevation can now be drawn.

The wings have been developed by, first of all, sectioning the body at F/1 and, to help determine the shape of the wing for the front view, it is necessary to know its length. From the study of a duck with its wings folded, it will be seen that the length of the wing appears to be from the shoulder almost to the tip of the tail but, when estimating the total length, an allowance must be made for the part of the wing from the shoulder to its junction with the body. This part is hidden from view when the wings are folded, but, when open, it is part of the overall visual length. So the length of the wing is the distance from the shoulder to a point near the tip of the tail, plus the distance from the shoulder to F/1. This must be plotted on the front view by projecting the point of connection of wing with body, and allowing the length of the wing to intersect with the projected line from the wing tip.

To draw a plan view, certain conclusions have been drawn from topographical study of the bird: a duck's head is thin, its neck is round and its body oval. At least that is the information this study is based on. It may not be true to nature but hopefully it will help make an interesting composition of form.

Dimensions for the plan view of the body have been taken from the elevation with allowances made to conform to the topographical observation. Where the body is oval, the dimension along the lines C/1, D/1 and E/1 in the elevation, have been increased approximately 25%. The neck at H/1 remains the same, whilst the head at I/1 was decreased a little. Drawing the true shape of the wing is quite simply projecting the intersecting points of the lines C/1, D/1, E/1, F/1 and G/1, with the wing in the elevation on to the front view, and then transferring these to intersect with C/1, D/1, E/1, F/1 and G/1.

The author realises that the understanding of the working drawings in this chapter will be difficult for some but, if the words tend to confuse, then a study of the projection lines may simplify comprehension. This illustration of the finished work may also add clarity (figure 7).

For the sculptor who intends to construct a bird with its wings open, a clay model based on the methods described for determining the shape will help considerably. The model may also be modified to suit the sculptor's own interpretation of the subject.

As with any animal study, a knowledge of anatomy is an advantage, and many facets of this will come to light during the carving. Light and shade from a picture can be conveyed to a

figure 7

carving as a contour which will indicate form and add interest to the finished work. One important point to remember is that it is not a scale model that is being produced. The subject-matter is the realisation of an imagined form, based on nature's gift of a model, combined with the skills and efforts of the sculptor.

16 Carving a Horse

Chapter 15 showed how to compose a model from pictures that were not of the correct size for direct copy. The subject was the horse, which is now being used as a practical example of carving in the round. The size chosen is that of the example on scaling, and the timber used is Purpleheart, a beautiful wood, but one that requires care in carving for fear of breaking: in other words it does not take too kindly to the use of the mallet when working the smaller sections.

The grain is vertical and in the direction of the legs. After cutting the block of wood to size, the elevation of the horse was transferred to the wood via a piece of carbon paper, with views of the front and rear also being transferred to their respective ends (figure 1).

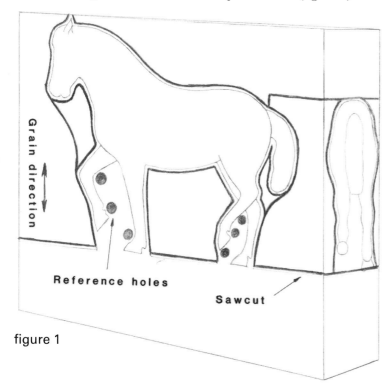

figure 1

Before cutting these profiles, the shape and possible problem areas were considered. The weakest parts are obviously the two legs which are raised off the ground. Another weak point is the junction of the tail with the body. The neck of the horse in the elevation looks substantial but, when considered with the front view, is in fact quite thin and is another not quite so obvious weak point.

The conclusions drawn were that the rough carving must be done before cutting away too much wood at or near the weaker places. Another problem was that, although cutting the elevation profile is straightforward, the depth of the wood is such that it is difficult to cut the profile right through for the front and rear of the horse. To overcome this difficulty, the front and back end sections of the profiled elevation were kept as templates. To give strength to the legs whilst roughing the carving, the wood between the fore and hind legs was left but, because the drawing of the legs will disappear whilst carving, reference holes were drilled through at points which made the delineation of the legs easier at a later stage.

The profile of the elevation was cut with a band saw, but a bow saw, or even the laborious use of a coping saw, would have been satisfactory. Cuts were approximately 2mm ($\frac{1}{16}$in.) from the line to allow for inaccurate cutting. The cut-off front and rear sections were also profiled in the other direction to provide templates (figure 2). An 18mm ($\frac{3}{4}$in.) no. 6 straight gouge was now used to cut the profiles to within 1mm ($\frac{1}{32}$in.) of the line, holding the block of wood in the vice. The front and rear sections were then held in their respective positions, with a piece of card under the base to raise them up to allow for the width of the saw cut, and the profiles drawn on to the body of the horse.

Roughing out the shape could now be started, but the sculptor who wanted reasonable accuracy or sensitivity in his model would realise that, with the pictures available, he still did not have enough information. The pictures he worked from were much too small to give the detail necessary for a good subject, but with the help of a local library, books on horses could be borrowed and sufficient information gleaned to show muscle detail and shape of face, legs, thighs etc. Although the exact pose of the horse being carved was not shown in the books, there was enough similarity in other poses to give an idea of shapes and style that would produce a natural and more interesting finished sculpture. Study of light and shade in the pictures acts as a guide to the depth and position of hollows, so necessary in the final shape.

From the original drawings made, the shape of the front of the horse was determined, but it must be realised that this is the front part only and extends no further than the front thighs. Beyond this point, the shape is related to the rear profile.

In starting the carving, the 18mm ($\frac{3}{4}$in.) no. 6 gouge was used with the mallet, to cut almost to the line and rough out the shape of the body and legs. It is as well to point out at this stage that when

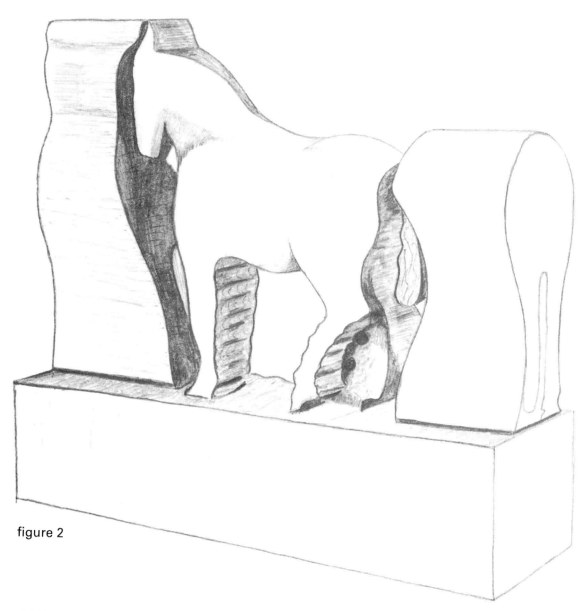

figure 2

dealing with the raised legs, care must be taken not to cut them free
of the base, otherwise, because of the short grain, there will not be
enough strength in the wood to withstand the force of the tools.

The shape of the body, haunches, legs and head was obtained
with the 18mm (¾in.) no. 6 gouge. To profile the legs, a 6mm
(¼in.) no. 10 straight gouge was used and, for working on the
underside of the legs, a bent 6mm (¼in.) gouge with no. 4 sweep,
while a back bent gouge with an 8mm (⁵⁄₁₆in.) wide no. 6 sweep
provided the versatility required to carve what might be
considered an awkward position.

When encountering problems with deciding the shape of the body, it is useful if a model is available as a guide, made from clay or plasticine. A simple wire armature can be formed as a support for the legs, which may be straight for this exercise. Any errors can then be rectified on the clay model before commencing work on the wood. Careful study of the pictures should give enough information to help model the clay (figure 3).

figure 3

With most of the waste wood cut away, the mallet was discarded temporarily for hand pressure, always using two hands, one to push and the other to guide the tool. The tools should be sharp and only enough pressure used to make them cut cleanly and easily.

The head, body and tail were now finish-carved and rifflers used for the final shaping (figure 4). The wood between the legs was now cut away, but not before the legs were redrawn to coincide with the reference holes that were previously drilled. The mallet was brought into play again for this separation of the legs (figure 5), but care was needed to avoid breaking them. Once the tool had broken through to the other side, hand pressure was used to pare away the wood to its final shape.

Holding the work in the vice by its base provided easy access for the carving tools. The only position which the vice could not comfortably accommodate was the underside, and this was overcome by holding the work on the lap (figure 6). In finishing the surface of the horse, abrasive papers and metal scrapers were used.

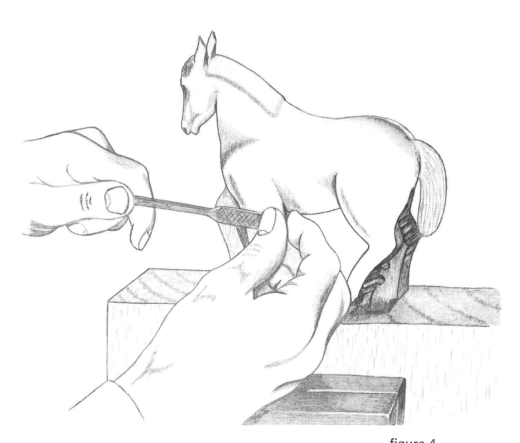

figure 4

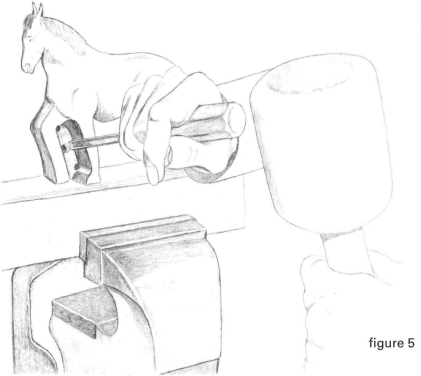

figure 5

105

figure 6

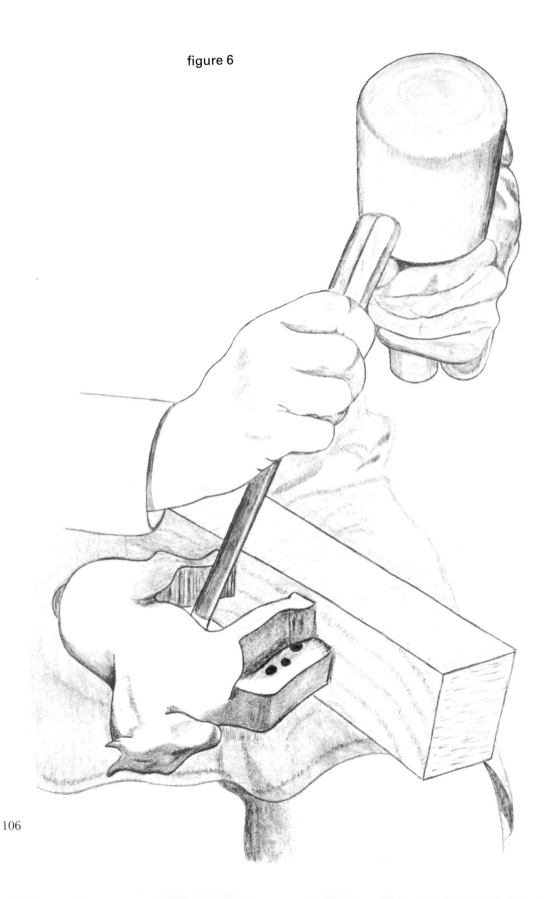

The surplus wood on the base was cut away, the base levelled and the sides sanded. The finished model was then sealed and wax polished.

One last piece of carving remained to be done, and that was to cut away the waste wood connecting the raised legs to the base. A carving knife was used for this, while the leg itself was supported by the fingers. The underside of the hooves was filed flat and sanded, as were the sides of the base. Note that the polishing was carried out before the raised hooves were cut free from the base. This was to prevent the pressure from the polishing cloth breaking the legs. Now all that remained was to seal and wax the underside of the hooves carefully: the finished horse may be seen in figure 7.

figure 7

17 Incised Carving

What has incised carving to do with wood sculpture? Incising is cutting into a surface, and it is a feature of detailed sculpture. The production of a sharp corner underneath the fold of a gown, for instance, or the facial or body features which necessitate a vee shaped cut, are all incised. The tools used for incising may be any one of the normal range of carving tools. Perhaps the most obvious one is the vee or parting tool, but its use is often dependent on the angle of tool that is available. In fact its performance in the following example would be limited by the complexity of the shape of the letters.

What is proposed in this section is to take the making of a house sign as a practical example, to show first of all how a task of this type is thought out and then to provide practice in the use of some of the carving tools.

Figure 1 is a photograph of the finished sign which was carved into a piece of oak 584mm (23in.) x 190mm (7½in.) x 25mm (1in.). The surface of the wood was planed to a smooth finish, but the edges were left until the carving was completed. This provided some protection in case the wood was inadvertently dropped.

figure 1

Choosing a typeface is a matter of personal preference and books on lettering and calligraphy usually have a choice of typefaces. The typeface selected for this sign is shown in figure 2, and the problem it presented was how to transfer the letters, which were illustrated as very small characters, on to the oak panel.

figure 2

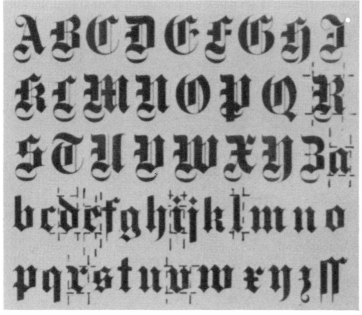

Boxing in the relevant letters, as shown in the figure, means that dimensions may be taken from these lines to position the construction lines. These facilitate the build up of each letter on the master, in this case the tracing paper shown on the drawing board in figure 3. Each letter has something in common with the other letters, and this shows up clearly when looking along the construction lines. What has been produced is a series of rectangles into which the relevant parts of each letter are drawn. The spacing of the letters is not constant, but varies with the shape of the preceding letter and, as there are no rules for this, it must be done visually. On the master, the letters were spaced directly on the drawing board but, if difficulty is encountered, each letter may be cut out and the spacing adjusted with the letter finally being fixed in place with clear adhesive tape. This method is described more fully in the next chapter, which discusses the relief carving of a house sign.

When the master is satisfactory, the letters have to be transferred to the timber. The name is centralised on the oak panel and held in place with adhesive tape (figure 4), and a piece of carbon paper is then slipped underneath before tracing each letter profile with a ball-point pen. A bench holdfast or 'G' clamps may be used for clamping the wood to the bench, but it is important to

109

figure 3

figure 4

place a piece of scrap wood or hardboard under the clamps to protect the surface of the wood panel.

Each letter now needs a centre line drawn on, together with the mitres at the corners (figure 5), and these lines are then punched in with the chisel, taking care at the mitres to hold the chisel at the correct angle (figures 6 and 7).

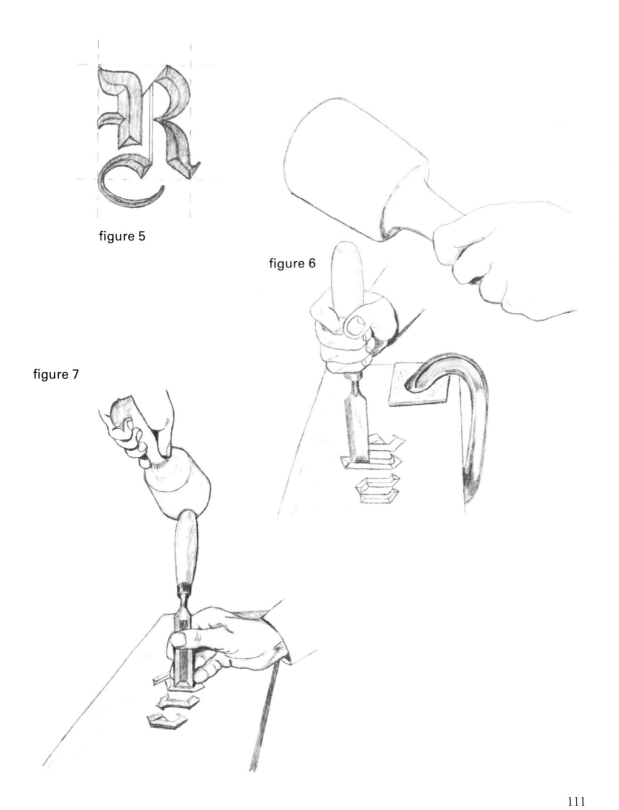

figure 5

figure 6

figure 7

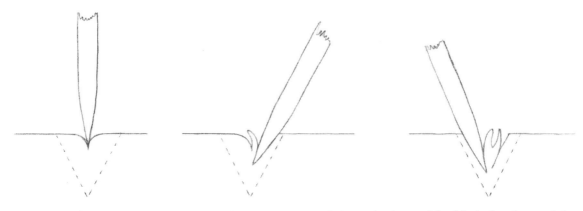

figure 8

Roughing out each letter is done with chisels for the straight sides, and gouges for the curved sides. The sequence of cuts is shown in the diagram (figure 8), but the cut stops short of the line by 1mm (1/32in.) to allow for finishing. Two things are important at this stage. One is that the angles at which the tool is held are fairly constant, and the other is not to cut the centre of the letter too deep. This is inclined to leave an unsightly groove along the centre line of the letter.

Often the same tools that were used for roughing out can also be used for the finishing but, in this instance, the skew chisel was used to afford practice with this tool. The slicing cut that it produces (figure 9) gives a nice finish and the shape of its cutting edge enables the mitres to be accommodated (figure 10). Because a back

figure 9

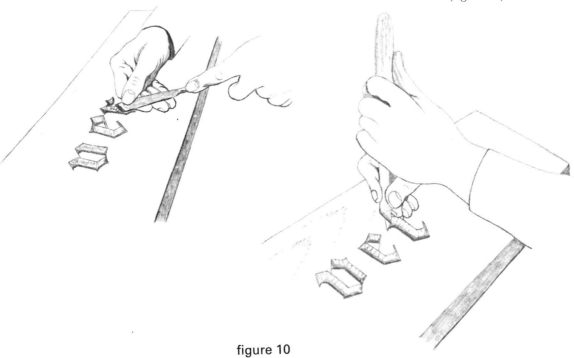

figure 10

112

bent gouge was not available for the convex sides of the letters, the roughing out was done with the 8mm (⁵⁄₁₆in.) no. 4 gouge (figure 11) and finished with the skew. The concave sides were finished with the gouges (figure 12).

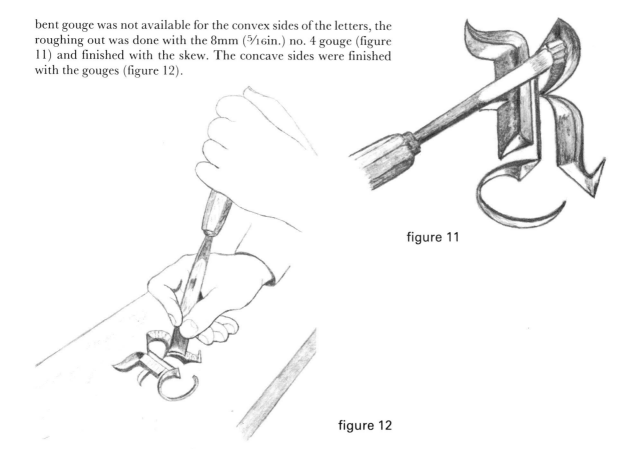

figure 11

figure 12

Throughout the carving a study of the grain direction is necessary, especially where slicing cuts have to be made along the angular parts of the letters. The cuts must be made in the direction of the slope of the grain to avoid the possibility of breaking away the edge of the wood.

With the carving finished, the panel was then cut to size, the edges planed square and the sharp corners rounded off with abrasive paper. There were some pencil marks left at the edges of the letters which were taken off with a sanding block. A sanding block is either a block of cork, or a wooden block with a cork face, around which abrasive paper is wrapped. The paper used was 220 grit garnet. Had the paper been held in the fingers, the edges of the letters might have become rounded.

The panel was to be displayed outdoors, so it was given two coats of exterior clear varnish which had been thinned with white spirit. The brush used was of good quality and care was taken to ensure that the varnish did not build up at the bottom of the letters. Between each coat of varnish, and when it was thoroughly dry, the face was flattened with *wet or dry* silicone carbide paper, 320 grit, used wet and wrapped around the sanding block. This cut back the surface to provide a nice flat key for the two subsequent coats of varnish which were not thinned down.

After the final coat, the surface was rubbed down, first with 600 and then 800 grit papers, used wet. The finished sign was then polished with a metal polish which gave perhaps too classical a finish for a house sign but it showed what can be achieved with clear varnishes.

Figure 13 shows the tools used in this example: 7mm (9/32in.) straight chisel (1), 25mm (1in.) firmer chisel (2), 18mm (3/4in.) no. 6 straight gouge (3), 18mm (3/4in.) no. 4 straight gouge (4), 8mm (5/16in.) no. 4 straight gouge (5) and 18mm (3/4in.) skew chisel (6).

figure 13

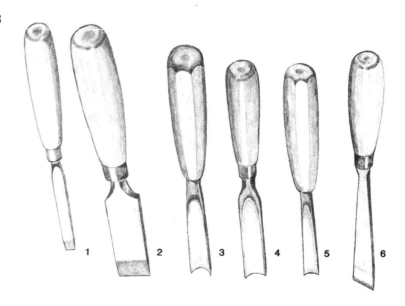

CHIP CARVING

Using the shape of the cutting edge of either a carving knife or carving tool, to produce a design in the surface of a piece of wood, is referred to as chip carving. The designs usually take the form of repeated geometric patterns and often require the tools to be ground to a shape which will accommodate the design.

The box (figure 14), which is of German or Swiss origin *c.*1500, is an example that was executed with the chisel and gouge. Another is the Tyrolean bottle stopper (figure 15). To produce attractive items for the tourists, the craftsman has used specially ground gouges to carve this head with the minimum of effort.

Chip carving, as far as wood sculpture is concerned, has its uses in the production of repetitive pieces and repetitive form. In other words, if there is enough demand to justify the reshaping of a tool, be it knife or carving tool, then expediency justifies this alteration, because it makes the work easier and more accurate.

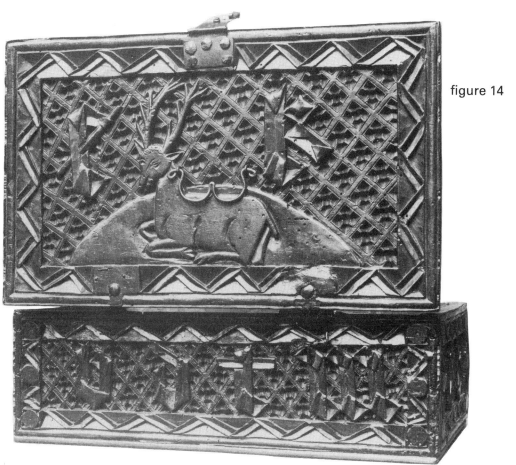

figure 14

figure 15

115

18 Relief Carving

When the background is carved away and the subject stands proud of the surface, the model is said to be in relief and, depending on the depth of the background, may be considered high or low relief.

Figure 1 shows a home sign made by a craftsman who specialises in this type of carving, and it is interesting to see how his work is both developed and executed. As an example of relief carving, this might be considered a relatively simple one, but its purpose here is to convey an idea which is functional, decorative and a good starting point for initiates of the craft.

figure 1

Designs used are the result of discussion between the craftsman and his client. Choice of typeface, layout of the sign and the form of embellishment, all have to be sorted out to satisfy both the client and high standards of the craftsman. To lend that touch of realism to the sign, research into the shape of the owl and the trailing leaves had to be carried out.

Timber for the signs is usually air dried home-grown hardwood approximately 25mm (1in.) thick. The example shown is made of elm. The moisture content of air seasoned timber is ideal for work which is to be sited outdoors and, when sealed with paint or varnish, usually remains stable.

Templates for the letters were produced by gluing photocopy enlargements of original typefaces to card and carefully profiling them. Because the baseline for the words of this sign is curved, each letter was arranged with its base tangential to this curve and, when positioned, was fixed in place with adhesive tape. The pattern detail was drawn full size on paper and transferred to the wood via carbon paper.

Clearing away the background was done with a power router and finished by hand with a gouge, although the gouge could have been used throughout.

Figure 2 shows the sign being worked, and the array of carving tools is the extent required, except for one straight 6mm (¼in.)

figure 2

veiner and a bent riffler. To give emphasis to the carving detail, the background was stained with spirit stain. This was carefully applied with an artist's brush around the relief to prevent the colour penetrating the upstanding sides. The finished sign was given several coats of exterior varnish.

The technique of relief carving is to create an impression of depth and for this it is imperative that the perspective of the drawing is correct. Depth is given to the carving by creating shadows in the same way that the artist treats his drawing or painting. The sculpture in figure 3, 'Salome and Zebedee', is a

figure 3

beautiful example of high relief by Tilmann Riemenschneider (1460–1531), the master of relief carving. Salome is carved in the round with disproportionate depth, while Zebedee is a much more shallow model in high relief. In works such as this, a sharp corner or undercut produces a dark shadow giving the impression of depth. This is shown by Zebedee's hand, where the fingers appear as if they were of full depth, when in actual fact they are quite shallow. The darker side of the fingers has been undercut whereas the other side has not.

An example of low relief is this carved table top in oak (figure 4). The thickness of the top is 19mm (¾in.) and the depth of the background 5mm (³⁄₁₆in.).

figure 4

figure 5

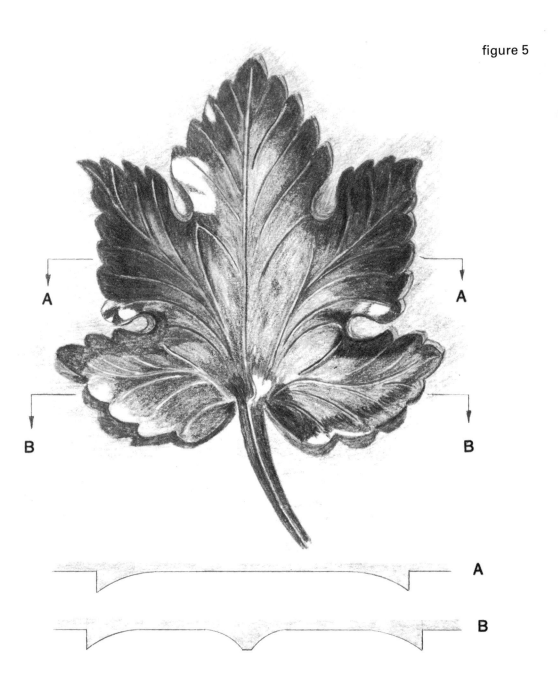

The first operation in relief work is to line in the subject. A parting tool cuts a shallow vee along the pencil lines to prevent them disappearing when carving commences. It is as well to start the carving at the most outstanding part of the subject – the part that is the farthest away from the background. There is always a very strong temptation to cut deeper, which must be resisted. Remember that it is not so much the depth of cut that gives the form its roundness, but rather the type of cut employed.

Looking at cross-sections of one of the leaves in the table top (figure 5), it will be seen that the edges of the leaf are square with the base. It is the shadow which creates the impression that the edge is separated from its background. Where the leaves curl, the radius is tighter and, as the diagram shows, the three-dimensional effect is created by light and shade. The dark shading and highlights in the drawing of the leaf indicate the upturned edges. Two cross-sectional views show the form of the leaf at A and B, to emphasise how necessary it is to study the picture when carving.

19 Whittling

'To love playthings well as a child, to lead an adventurous and honourable youth and to settle when the time arrives into a green and smiling age is to be a good artist and deserves well of yourself and your neighbour'
Robert Louis Stevenson

One of the aims of this book is to convey to others the pleasure that comes from a hobby which embraces different techniques, and which can be enjoyed by young and old alike. It requires only moderate outlay and has the advantage of providing fulfilment in the comfort of the home.

Whittling is wood carving that uses the technique of holding the workpiece in one hand and the tools in the other. It is usually associated with using knives, but there are occasions when woodcarving tools are required. As an activity to be engaged in at home, it provides an opportunity to work within the family unit.

An example of a carved bird will be discussed here in detail. It has been chosen because it employs a number of techniques which have been mentioned previously in this book.

The avocet (figure 1), with its upturned bill, is a summer visitor to the shallow waters of East Anglia, and carving it presents a problem to the sculptor which is related to its construction rather than to the carving. The slender beak, were it straight, would not be very strong but the additional problem of the curve presents a seemingly impossible task. One way of dealing with the difficulty would be to make the beak from metal, in the same way as the legs, but another, more effective method is to laminate the wood, bend the end and glue the whole together.

There are three views of the avocet. The timber used for the body is jelutong; an easily worked wood that is used largely in the engineering industry for pattern making. Easy workability is one reason for this choice of wood, but the main reason is the fact that the character of the wood is ideal for pyrography. It has very little grain pattern to influence the texture burnt on with the pyrography pen.

The following is a brief description of the making up of the bird assisted by line diagrams.

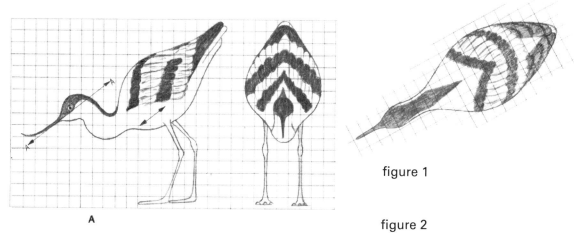

A

figure 1

figure 2

Thickness of timber used is 75mm (3in.), and the first operation is to mark off the profile of the bird as shown in figure 2 (A). It will be seen from the line AA that the head is a separate piece of wood, therefore it is only the body which has to be drawn on to the wood. The profile is now cut and attention turned to the beak. This was made from parana pine but any straight-grained timber would be suitable.

From the diagram, it will be seen that the beak has been developed from wood which has the grain running along its length. This thin piece of wood has been split down the centre, bent with the aid of steam and then glued together. The fibrous structure of the wood changes on bending, with compression and tension forces in each layer being retained by bonding the layers together. The new shape of the beak develops remarkable strength, but the retention of the curved form of the beak requires 'formers' – specially shaped pieces of wood to hold the split beak together whilst the glue sets.

The profile of the beak is marked on to the pine block (B) making sure that the grain is parallel to the straight part of the beak. The dotted line is a continuation of the thickest part of the beak. The beak is profiled and the parallel dotted lines indicate the 6mm (¼in.) width of the beak, which also has to be cut, before splitting with the knife (C). The split extends to the front of the head.

Two formers (D), made from scrap wood approximately 18mm (¾in.) thick and shaped to accommodate the form of the beak, are required to hold the bent beak in position whilst the glue sets, but

figure 3

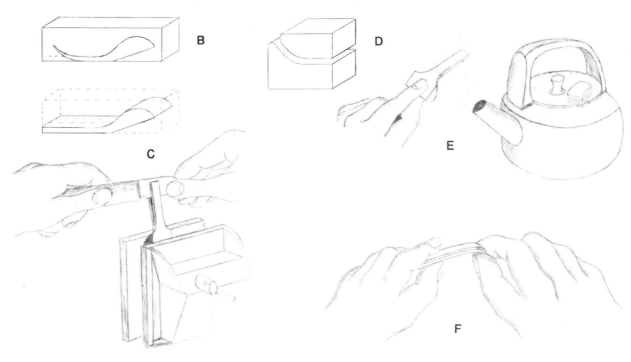

B

C

D

E

F

124

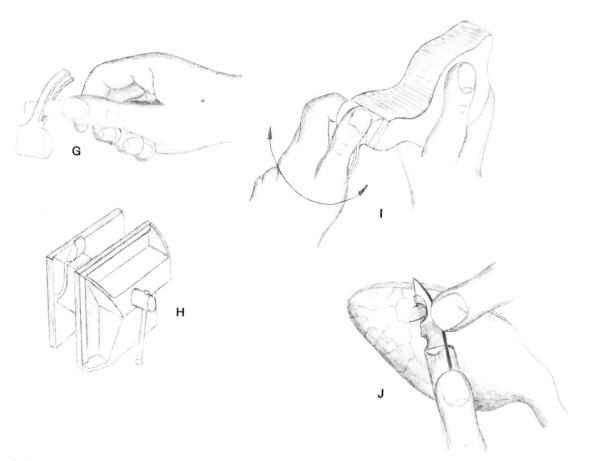

figure 4

before these can be used, steam has to be applied to soften the wood for bending. A folded cloth, placed over the lid vent, directs the steam through the spout of a kettle and the beak is either held in the steam (E) or pushed into the spout. It takes from five to ten minutes of steaming for the wood to become pliable enough to conform to the shape of the former. The fingers are used to bend the wood (F) and glue is inserted into the split of the beak with thin card pushing the glue up as far as possible (G), before wrapping in polythene to prevent the adhesion of the beak to the former. (Polythene wrapping will exclude the air and prevent polyvinyl acetate glue from setting, so it is important that one side of the wrapping remains open.) Clamping the assembly in the vice for twenty-four hours (H) allows the glue to cure and the beak to take on a permanent set. Fixing the head to the body requires two flat surfaces which are glued and wrung together (I).

After sawing to the plan profile, carving can be started using the knife (J) to clear away most of the waste and undercutting the wings and tail (K). To create the appearance of ruffled feathers at the breast and shoulders, a flat gouge, say a no. 3, is used to carve

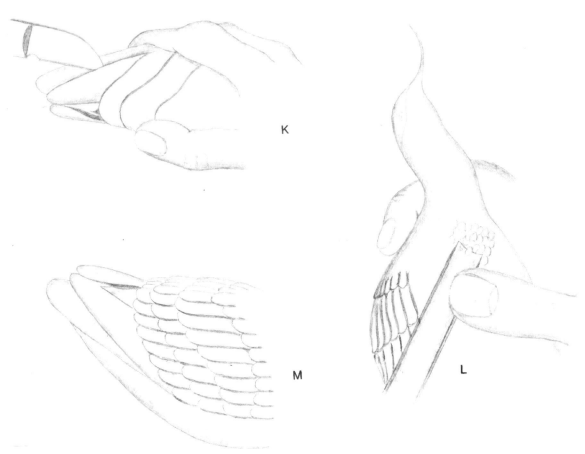

figure 5   hollows (L) but the carving of the feathers on the back (M) is the work of the knife, parting tool and gouge.

Shaping the beak is the last of the carving operations. In fact, the body of the bird is finally shaped, scraped and sanded before the beak is touched. As the most delicate feature of the carving, much care must be exercised with this part. Small pieces at a time are pared away and the thumb used to control the cut. A roll of fine abrasive paper is used to give the beak its final shape, but care has to be taken to avoid sanding away too much.

The black feathers are emphasised with the pyrography pen (N). Using the side of the tip to burn deep, narrow grooves, an impression is created which compares favourably with the real bird.

The base of the bird is simply a piece of polished hardwood of random shape, and the bird is mounted so that the base extends beyond the beak to provide some protection for this delicate part (0).

The legs of this bird are made of 2.5mm (³/₃₂in.) steel rod, and are bent to follow the pattern of the drawing plus about 25mm (1in.), which penetrates the body, and another 12mm (½in.) to go into the base.

figure 6

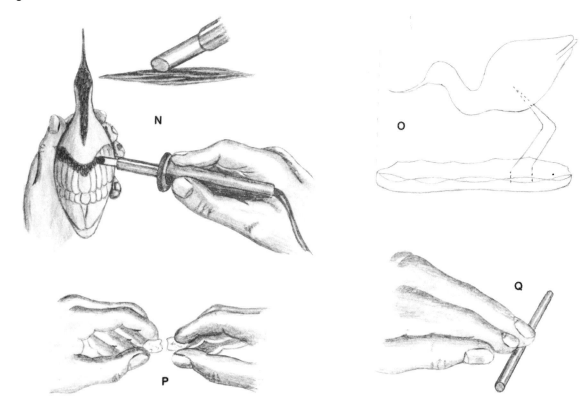

N

O

P

Q

Epoxy adhesive is used to bond the legs, but not before the ends
of the steel are abraded with a coarse abrasive paper to form a key.
When the adhesive has hardened, epoxy resin in the form of putty
is used to model the thighs, knee joints and feet. N.B.: always read
and follow the manufacturer's advice when using these resins. The
resin and hardener (P) which make up this putty have to be
kneaded together (Q) and it is advisable to make up only small
quantities at a time because the material hardens very quickly.
Epoxy adhesive is used as an additional aid to bonding the putty to
the steel, but cleaning and abrading of the steel also helps
adhesion. Tools for modelling the resin may be made from bent
wire (R) or, if the sculptor has a friendly dentist, he might possibly
obtain from him some of the tools he used for filling and scraping
teeth (S) which are ideal.

The diagrams show how the putty is applied (T). The idea is to
create an impression and not a scale model of the joint. Any surplus
material may be filed away after the resin has hardened. Modelling
the feet (U) of the avocet, requires first of all scratching through the
polish of the base to provide a key for the adhesive. This may be
done with the point of the carving knife, before a very fine bead of

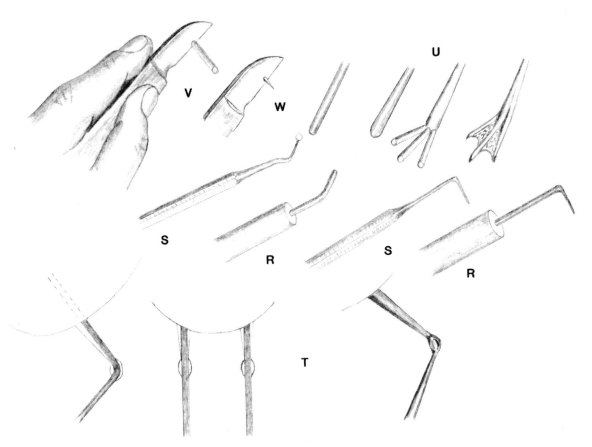

figure 7   epoxy adhesive is applied with a pointed stick. The fingers are used to roll sausages of putty to make the toes, which are then cut to length with a knife. The fact that they stick to the blade helps with the positioning (V). Claws are comparatively easy to form and position, but it is necessary to let the toes harden first. The point of a roll of putty is cut off (W) and transferred to the toe to be pressed home with the tool.

When the epoxy adhesive and putty have hardened, the surplus may be scraped away (it will not stick to any polished surface) and any detail may be put in with files.

Painting the legs is the final operation, and the idea is to choose a colour that suits the carving, and not one that copies the natural colouring of the bird. Should the paint touch the polished surface, wait until it dries, and then gently scrape it away with a knife.

20 Finishing Techniques

The finish given to a piece of sculpture is an integral part of the work. It has a message to convey in addition to its function as a protective coating. There are various types of finish and various reasons for their use. Primarily, the finish should form a protection against the ingress of moisture and dirt, but running a close second is emphasis. Wood with a beautiful grain pattern does not look quite so spectacular before it is polished as it does afterwards, when emphasis is placed on the grain.

A carving which has a lot of detail requires a tremendous amount of effort, sandpapering and scraping to prepare it for polishing. What the sculptor must ask himself is how far to take the finishing process. It may well be that the form is all that he wants to convey so that any finish other than that left by the carving tool would be a waste of time.

When art is combined with craftsmanship, examples with tremendous impact may be the result. Figure 4 on p. 80 of Barbara Hepworth's 'Pelagos' is a fine example, where emphasis has been given to the form in a number of ways with polished surfaces, painted areas, tooled finish and the geometric suggestion of the strings coupled with fine craftsmanship.

Church carvings, such as the ends of pews and choir stalls (shown at Winchester Cathedral in figure 1), were originally left untreated. The flowers, foliage or other design was carved and then left with the tool marks showing. The sheen or patina on the wood is the result of many years of being handled, i.e. the tactile effect. The grain of the wood has become filled with natural oils and wax from cleaning materials. Now why did the carver leave only a tooled finish instead of a nicely polished one? The work was possibly a portrayal of a Biblical story, or maybe symbolic of a particular theme, so there was no need to bring out the beauty of the wood by polishing. The carving was the focal point and not the grain of the wood.

'The Cormorants' by William Graveney (figure 1 p. 85) is an example of tooled finish where the form of the birds is the primary factor. Here again, the sculptor could see no reason to extend the

figure 1

finishing process beyond the shape he wished to convey. The stance of the birds, with a suggestion of movement, gives the sculpture life. The finish creates another aspect and turns the work into a conversation piece. Imagination on the part of the viewer comes into play and questions are asked. Why did the sculptor not give his work a finer finish? Is this a sketch model for a larger work? Were the models bedraggled from leaving the sea and is this tooled finish meant to convey this appearance? The answer to these questions is that they are unimportant. The artist should be judged by the form he has created and not always by the craftsmanship alone.

Polishing wood is a process which first of all seals the grain of the wood and then leaves a smooth film on the surface. Before any polishing can be carried out, however, the timber must be prepared. Consider what happens when a piece of timber has been cut with a very sharp tool, such as a plane. The surface of the wood feels very smooth because the cells or fibres have been cut through cleanly by the tool. The wood is dampened with water and left to dry. The surface of the wood now becomes rough, because the fibres have swelled and risen above the surface. If very fine abrasive paper is now rubbed along this surface, the fibres are levelled and the wood becomes smooth again.

This raising of the grain is a necessary part of all polishing. Either the dampening process is repeated until the roughness felt on drying has gone or a grain filler is used. Grain fillers were traditionally Plaster of Paris, rubbed into the grain with a coarse damp cloth, but nowadays proprietary fillers have the advantage of being cleaner to use and transparent. Whereas the Plaster of Paris left minute white flecks in the wood, the modern fillers take on the colour of the wood. Another way of filling the grain is to use the polish itself, if it has a shellac base. Any moisture applied will cause the grain to lift up, and the actual polishing must be carried out on a smooth surface, which indicates that light sanding is required between each coat.

POLISHING

For the purposes of this book, the materials used are proprietary products and a list of suppliers will be found in the appendix.

French Polishing

French polishing is the deposition of a thin film of shellac on to the surface of the wood via a solvent of methylated spirit. It gives a beautiful finish, but has the disadvantage of highlighting any defects in the timber. Extreme care must be taken in the preparation of the wood to remove any scratches or marks from either the tools or the abrasive papers.

The grain should first of all be filled with either the polish itself or a grain filler. If grain filler is used, the method of application is to rub the paste into the wood with a cloth, working across the grain, to force the filler into the open grain. The surplus may be wiped away along the grain. Allow a minimum of three-four hours for the filler to dry before sandpapering the surface and clearing away the dust.

French polish is applied with a rubber, which is made from a pad of cotton wool or wadding about 100mm (4in.) square lying on a piece of linen about 200mm (8in.) square. Polish is poured into the centre of the pad (figure 2) and the corners folded over to trap the liquid. The corners of the linen square are then twisted together (figure 3) forcing the polish through the face of the linen (figure 4) which is then applied to the wood. The rubber is moved over the surface of the wood with a circular motion, gradually covering the whole area. The polish must not be allowed to ooze through the linen – the idea is to allow only enough polish through to cover the surface evenly. Once the surface has been evenly covered, it should be left to dry and harden for 24 hours before the next application

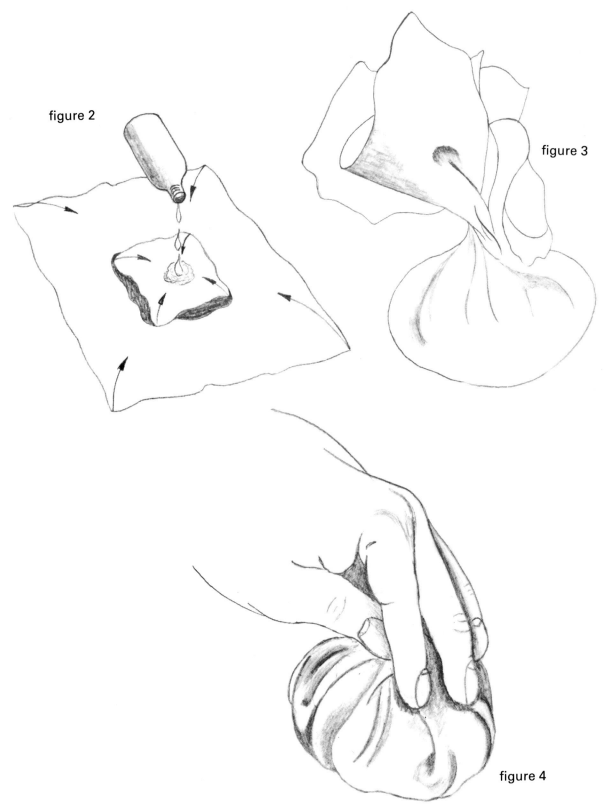

figure 2

figure 3

figure 4

132

of polish. The rubber should be kept in an airtight container to keep it soft and ready for use.

Awkward areas in sculpture may require the rubber to be shaped to fit, a smaller rubber made or even the application of polish with a brush (known as a polishing mop). The degree of polish depends on the number of coats given and the care with which they are applied. Between each coat, the surface is rubbed down with 400 grit abrasive paper to give a smooth, even surface.

As the polish builds up on the surface of the wood, the rubber has a tendency to stick or drag. The rapid evaporation of the solvent leaves a sticky layer of shellac on the wood and, if the rubber is dragged across this, the surface could be spoiled. To lubricate the rubber and prevent this happening, a small amount of linseed oil is applied to the rubber, usually dabbed on with the finger. When applying subsequent coats, the amount of polish should be gradually reduced, as an excess of polish will soften and ruin previous coats. After, say, three coats of polish, the rubber may be rubbed in the direction of the grain of the wood instead of using a circular motion.

The work should finally be left for a few days to harden, and then rubbed with a clean rubber which has been slightly dampened with methylated spirit, to remove the linseed oil and impart the final finish.

Wax Polish

Wax polish is quite simply a layer of wax which has been allowed to harden and then burnished with a cloth. The surface of the sculpture must again be free from tool marks or scratches from the sandpaper before any finish can be applied. It is an advantage to give the work one or two coats of french polish or other shellac based liquid polishes before the wax is applied. This has the advantage of raising the grain and filling it before being cut back with 400 grit abrasive paper.

There are various types of wax polishes available, but the type recommended here is the soft white wax, which should be applied with very fine steel wool of grade 0000. A wad of steel wool is dipped into the polish and a generous amount rubbed into the wood, taking care to work in the direction of the grain. Surplus polish is wiped off with a cloth and the workpiece left for 24 hours for the wax to harden. A soft polishing cloth is now rubbed vigorously over the surface to bring up the lustrous finish given by this type of polish.

Shoe Polish

Shoe polish is another medium which produces good results, especially on dense hardwoods such as rosewood, beech, etc. It should be applied in the same way as wax polish.

OILED FINISH

Oiled finishes are used by some craftsmen, their effectiveness and ease of application being the inducement which overcomes the period of weeks which is the time it may take for the oil to dry.

The oil is a mixture of 60% linseed oil and 40% pure turpentine and it is applied by vigorous rubbing into the pores of the wood with a soft cloth. The wood will only absorb so much oil at each application, so the surplus is wiped away before the work is finally rubbed with a clean cloth. It is important that the oil is dry before the next coat is applied. Since the oil will raise the grain, it is necessary to rub down lightly between coats with 400 grit abrasive paper.

Sculpted dishes which are to be used for food are treated with vegetable oil, and, when in use, should never be immersed in water but wiped over with an oiled cloth before storage.

figure 5

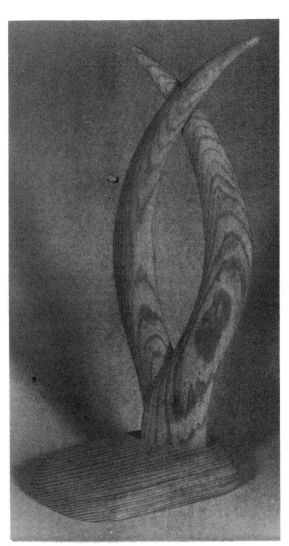
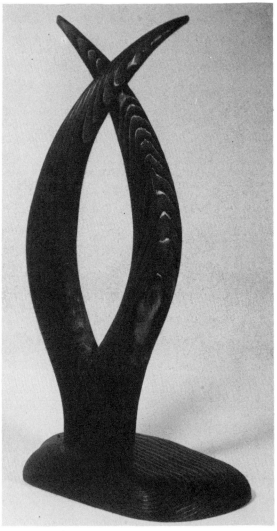

TEXTURED FINISHES

Scorched and Wire Brushed

Scorched and wire brushed is a finish which gives an extraordinary effect, especially on softwoods such as Douglas fir. Figure 5 is a simple example where the carved form was sandpapered smooth and then severely burnt with a blowlamp. When the charred wood was brushed away, the effect is to give a third dimension to the grain of the wood. The softer spring growth is eroded to a greater depth than that of the denser summer wood. The carving shown in figure 5 is of Douglas fir and gives an indication of the extent of burning required.

To clear away the charred wood, an engineer's wire brush is used, always brushing in the direction of the grain of the wood. Soft brass wire brushes of the type used for suede shoes are also useful but, for small awkward corners, small brushes can be made at home, using a few wire bristles taken from a brass brush and binding them to a piece of wooden dowelling with fuse wire.

The subject chosen for this exercise presented a few areas where precautions had to be taken against burning away some of the shape. As the edges of the form are very thin, the timber would have very little resistance to the heat from the blowlamp. Fireclay was used to line the underside of every edge where it was important to retain the shape, before applying the flame.

Pyrography

Pyrography, or to use the old fashioned term 'poker work', is a technique which is enjoying a revival. The advent of electrical burning tools has meant that the artist has control over the extent to which the surface of the wood may be textured. The author's carved birds are examples of this technique.

The sculpture is prepared for pyrography in the same way as for polishing. One might imagine that any scratches left in the wood would be burnt away, but in fact, unless the surface is severely burnt, any scratches or marks on the surface will still show.

There is a variety of pyrography pens on the market and they all have their uses, but the one used for the birds shown is a type which looks very much like a soldering iron. The illustration (figure 6) shows the tip used by the author, but different tips are also available. It takes a little practice to control such an unwieldy tool, but in essence it is just like drawing with a pencil, only much slower. The edge of the tip does most of the work, cutting into the surface of the wood, and a variety of effects can be obtained by working the tool across the grain of the wood or along it.

Wood which has been burnt with a pyrography pen requires an ultra-violet light inhibitor in the polish, as the burnt markings tend to fade if exposed to strong natural light. The polish provides a certain amount of protection against this but, even so, fading will occur. It is advisable to keep sculptures finished in this way in a shaded recess or display cabinet. Another point is to design the

figure 6

sculpture so that it is the form which is the important feature and not the pyrography, which will fade.

Tool Finishing

A tooled finish is that obtained by the carving tools only. The example by Tilmann Riemenschneider (figure 3 p. 118) has infinite complexity of form, and all the surfaces of this carving show delicate marks from the carving tools. The fine detail in this masterpiece could only be produced with the carving tools.

When a tooled finish is used, it is essential to get the shape or form right before starting on the finishing. Only light cuts should be made with the finishing gouge, each of roughly the same size and each overlapping the last cut made.

PAINTING

Painting is an acceptable way of finishing sculpture, which reflects the care and interest of the craftsman. A slapdash finish is indicative of slapdash work, but a good finish indicates that thought and care have gone into the whole project.

Surface preparation is as for the polished finishes. The first coat of paint should be primer, which is left to dry and then rubbed down with silicone carbide paper to remove any brush marks. A good quality brush should be used to leave as few brush marks as possible. *Wet or dry* paper (say 280 grit) used wet, is very effective, but care must be taken not to wet any part of the work which is to be left unpainted, as the timber may be affected. The undercoat is then applied and rubbed down before finishing with a top coat of gloss paint. The best finish is obtained if the top coat is also rubbed down with 400 and then 600 *wet or dry* paper (used wet), to produce a fine, even surface which may then be polished with metal polish to return a matt or high gloss finish.

Polychrome is the term used for multicoloured sculpture. With some very detailed sculptures, it would not be possible to rub down and paint in the manner described, neither is it necessary nor advisable to use the colouring agents used by the sculptors of history. Modern watercolours, such as poster paints or gouache, make good grounds for finishing over with wax. Enamel paints are also good colour media but they do require fine quality brushes.

DRAWING INKS

Drawing inks work very well on wood and may be applied by brush or pen. Colour variations may be made by mixing the inks, or diluting the colour by adding distilled water. There is no problem with colours running together, as the ink dries very quickly.

Suppliers

TOOL SUPPLIERS

Rogers Tools
47 Walsworth Road
HITCHEN
Herts SG4 9SU

Ashley Iles (Edge Tools) Ltd
East Kirkby
SPILSBY
Lincolnshire PE23 4DD

Henry Taylor Tools Ltd
The Forge
Lowther Road
SHEFFIELD S6 2DR

Alec Tiranti Ltd
70 High Street
THEALE
Berkshire

Sargents Tools
45-52 Oxford Road
READING
Berkshire RG1 7LH

or, for overseas orders

Sargents Tools Overseas Ltd
Thorn Street
READING
Berkshire RG1 7LH

Woodcraft
P.O. Box 4000
41 Atlantic Avenue
WOBURN
Massachusetts 01888
U.S.A.

Constantine
2050 Eastchester Road
Bronx
NEW YORK 10461
U.S.A.

WOOD FINISHING PRODUCTS

House of Harbru
101 Crostons Road
Elton
BURY
Lancashire BL8 1AL

John Myland Ltd
80 Norwood High Street
LONDON SE27 9NW

Liberon Waxes
6 Park Street
LYDD
Kent

Gaston Wood Finishes
Department NC
P.O. Box 1246
3630 East 10th Street
BLOOMINGTON
In. 47401
U.S.A.

PYROGRAPHY TOOLS

Fred Aldous Ltd
P.O. Box 135
37 Lever Street
MANCHESTER M60 1UX

Ashley Iles Ltd
East Kirkby
SPILSBY
Lincolnshire PE23 4DD

Janik Wood Crafts
Brickfield Lane
Denbigh Road
RUTHIN
CLYWD, North Wales

Wood Craft
P.O. Box 4000
41 Atlantic Avenue
WOBURN
Massachusetts 01888
U.S.A.

ADHESIVES

Borden (UK) Ltd
North Baddesley
SOUTHAMPTON
Hampshire

ABRASIVES

English Abrasives Ltd
Marsh Lane
LONDON N17 0XA

Further Reading

Kettless, A. *Decorative Woodwork,* Evans Bros Ltd, London
Naylor, R. *Woodcarving Techniques,* B.T. Batsford Ltd, London
Tangerman, E.J. *Whittling and Woodcarving,* Dover Publications Inc., New York
Wheeler, W. and Hayward, C. *Practical Woodcarving and Gilding,* Evans Bros Ltd, London
Zanker, F.O. *Foundation Design in Wood,* Dryad Press, Leicester

MAGAZINES

Woodworker
published by: Model and Allied Publications Ltd
P.O. Box 35
Wolsey Road
HEMEL HEMPSTEAD
Hertfordshire HP2 4SS

Practical Woodworking
published by: I.P.C. Magazines Ltd
Kings Reach Tower
Stamford Street
LONDON SE1 9LS

Index